Praise for
Reset

"In every generation God raises up voices that speak with boldness and clarity the freedom found only in Jesus. Nick Hall is one of those voices. *Reset* stirred my own heart again to believe God for an awakening in our nation. When a generation can see Jesus for who he truly is, their lives will be reset and never the same."

—Banning Liebscher, founder and pastor of Jesus Culture and author of *Rooted: The Hidden Places Where God Develops You*

"Nick Hall has prayed big prayers and seen God answer in big ways. His story and the stories presented in *Reset* will give you the faith to truly believe Jesus changes everything. You are one prayer away from a reset life."

—Mark Batterson, *New York Times* best-selling author of *The Circle Maker* and lead pastor of National Community Church

"I love the message Nick shares in this book because we all have times we need to reset—to commit ourselves to the only One who can change us from the inside out. So whether you've been saved for one day or have had a relationship with Jesus for decades, *Reset* will give you the courage to go even further into intimacy with our King."

—Kari Jobe, singer/songwriter

"Nick Hall is dreaming of a generation reset, and I love working with people who dream big! I am so excited about the message of *Reset,* as I have seen first-hand that Jesus changes everything! Read this book and let the movement begin in us."

—Christine Caine, evangelist, author, and founder of the A21 Campaign

"Nick Hall has a heart that is passionate for God. He desperately wants people to come to know Jesus Christ and experience a reset in their lives. And that's what this book is all about."

—Steve Douglass, president of Cru

"God is using Nick Hall to call our generation to reset our lives in every way. His vision is large, his passion is contagious, and his energy is endless. Nick Hall believes that now is the time for a reset in America. I am believing God with him!"

—Dr. Ronnie Floyd, president of the Southern Baptist Convention and senior pastor at Cross Church

"I remember thinking the first time I played a PULSE college event with Nick Hall, *You can't miss that he is passionate about reaching this generation with the message of Jesus Christ.* I have no doubt *Reset* will leave an undeniable mark for the gospel."

—TobyMac, seven-time Grammy winner

"Nick Hall has powerfully put into words an invitation to a journey that is fun to read, overwhelmingly convicting, and accessible. The only thing more persuasive than the simple message of this book is Nick himself. He is a leader of deep conviction, Spirit-filled wisdom, an all-in attitude toward Jesus, and a lovable persona—all of this is captured vividly in the pages of *Reset.*"

—York Moore, national evangelist for InterVarsity Christian Fellowship USA

"Jesus is with you in the pain, the struggle, and the unbearable, holding you close and offering you a way out. In Nick Hall's timely book, *Reset,* you'll find the courage to crawl out of despair and into the arms of Jesus, and you'll find practical advice to live daily in his grace."

—Michael W. Smith, singer/songwriter

"Welcome to the land of beginning again. *Reset* tells the stories of starting over and invites us to our second chance."

—Leith Anderson, president of the National Association of Evangelicals and author of *Faith in the Voting Booth*

RESET

NICK HALL

FOREWORD BY
JOSH MCDOWELL AND LUIS PALAU

RESET

JESUS CHANGES EVERYTHING

MULTNOMAH

RESET

Details in some anecdotes and stories have been changed to protect the identities of the persons involved.

Trade Paperback ISBN 978-1-60142-912-4
Hardcover ISBN 978-1-60142-908-7
eBook ISBN 978-1-60142-909-4

Cover design by David Nanda

The author is represented by Alive Communications Inc., 7680 Goddard Street, Suite 200, Colorado Springs, Colorado 80920, www.aliveliterary.com.

Published in the United States by Multnomah, an imprint of the Crown Publishing Group, a division of Penguin Random House LLC, New York.

Library of Congress has cataloged the hardcover edition as follows:
Names: Hall, Nick (Evangelist), author.
Title: Reset : Jesus changes everything / Nick Hall.
Description: First Edition. | Colorado Springs, Colorado : Multnomah Books, 2016. | Includes bibliographical references.
Identifiers: LCCN 2016000392 | ISBN 9781601429087 (hardcover) | ISBN 9781601429094 (electronic)
Subjects: LCSH: Evangelistic work. | Revivals. | Change—Religious aspects—Christianity. | Change (Psychology)—Religious aspects—Christianity.
Classification: LCC BV3790 .H29 2016 | DDC 269/.2—dc23 LC record available at http://lccn.loc.gov/2016000392

2018

147506545

To my bride and best friend, Tiffany,
and to the generation that will change the world.
Buckle up. This is going to be fun.

My mouth will tell of your righteous deeds,
    of your saving acts all day long—
    though I know not how to relate them all.
I will come and proclaim your mighty acts, Sovereign LORD;
    I will proclaim your righteous deeds, yours alone.
Since my youth, God, you have taught me,
    and to this day I declare your marvelous deeds.
Even when I am old and gray,
    do not forsake me, my God,
till I declare your power to the next generation,
    your mighty acts to all who are to come.

PSALM 71:15–18, NIV

Contents

Foreword

In the 1970s, a movement known as Jesus People swept the nation as tens of thousands of hippies and drug addicts turned in their needles for Bibles, their skepticism for devotion, and their partying for praise. It was an amazing time in North American history as young people turned to faith in God en masse, causing even *Time* magazine to take note. "The Jesus Generation" was front-cover news, and an entire age group was positively changed. We have prayed for another such movement today.

The apostle Paul once told his protégé Timothy, "Don't let anyone look down on you because you are young, but set an example for the believers in speech, in conduct, in love, in faith and in purity" (1 Timothy 4:12, NIV). If we are to see a move of God today, it will only come about as new leaders rise up and embody those words of the apostle Paul. People like you. People like Nick Hall.

As you read Nick's story in *Reset,* you can be confident that this is not simply the story of a gifted young man from North Dakota. It is also the story of God himself who is changing lives. Through PULSE and the message of *Reset,* Nick has shared the gospel across the country before live audiences of millions of students, and to date more than five hundred thousand of those young women and young men have publicly responded to Jesus. God is moving in this generation! We see it across the globe and right here in the United States.

Our prayer for you, as you make your way through this book, is that your life would be the *next one changed.* Each one of us has given our life for the very message embodied in these pages, which is that Jesus really does change everything. Whatever you need reset in your life can be changed here and now, today, through the life-saving message of Jesus Christ.

Joyfully and gratefully,
Josh McDowell
Luis Palau

PART I

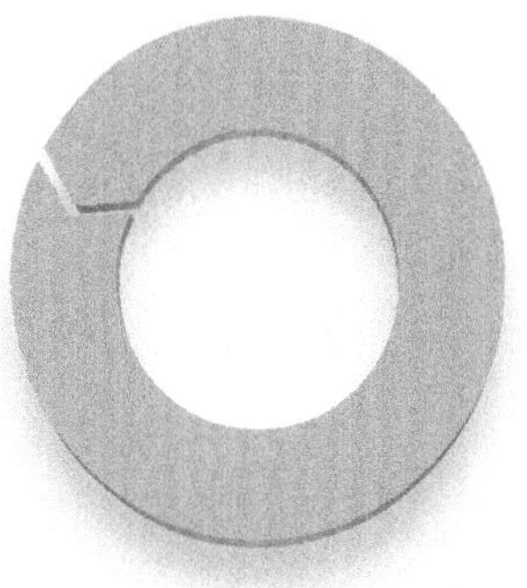

The Setup

Living the Dream

"Are you the guy from North Dakota doing the big youth events?" It was Billy Graham talking. As in, *the* Billy Graham. And he was talking to *me.* I thought I might pass out like a fangirl at a Justin Bieber concert. I was sitting in the living room of a living legend, and he—Dr. Graham—was making mention of PULSE, the ministry I had started. This had to be a dream, or a continuation of one, anyway.

The dream started becoming reality for me just before my freshman year of college, and by the time I was a junior, it was consuming my life. I'd been part of a few campus clubs by then and had met other students who were trying their best to live for Jesus and wanted to have an impact at our school. In addition, I would often have conversations with friends after class and learn that whenever they surveyed the climate of our campus, they were just as disheartened as I was. It seemed students were drunk all the time, or high, or both. They were harming themselves and destroying their lives. A few of them even committed suicide. Depression and despair were rampant; something had to give.

A few of those buddies and I decided to start meeting together every week to pray for our campus. We had no idea how our group was supposed to address the problems we were witnessing, but we believed that if we prayed and were willing to do what God said, he just might use us.

During the same season, my English prof assigned our class a project: write a fifteen-page business proposal and prepare a fifteen-minute presentation for the class on some change we wanted to see on campus. She divided the twenty-four or so students into groups of four and left it up to the groups to determine their project.

My school, North Dakota State University, was a pretty big party school. One of those designated party areas was the tailgating lot near the football stadium, but because there were more drinkers than the limited real estate could accommodate on game days, there had been a push for a bigger lot. My group for that English project decided this was its cause. The passionate plea? "Make Room for Our Beer!" I suppose the fight for justice takes on a variety of forms.

Another group would appeal for more parking on campus and still another for an on-campus golf course. And while these causes were fine by me, I came away from that class feeling unsatisfied. God had already given me a vision for seeing the campus changed by Jesus, and I wondered if forcing myself to formalize a specific strategy might help me actualize that goal. Instead of heading home after class, I waited for my professor to free up.

When I asked her if it would be okay for me to do the assignment on my own instead of in the context of a group, she looked perplexed. "It would be a lot more work to do it that way," she said, making sure I had counted the cost. "But if you're convinced that's what you want to do, then have at it. I'll give you the same presentation slot—fifteen minutes—but I'll need the same-length proposal from you . . . fifteen pages. Agreed?"

I sat down at my keyboard that night wondering what I'd gotten myself into. "God, I could use some help here," I prayed. "For starters, how do I even write a proposal?"

There was only one other person in that English class who I knew was involved in a campus ministry, but I'd take any help I could get. I pulled her aside after class one day and explained what I was going to do my presentation on. I asked her to pray for me between now and then. After all, I was going to be presenting a proposal to my classmates about reaching them. I could just hear myself: "Today, I want to talk to you about a big problem on our campus . . . you need Jesus!" Yeah, this was going to go over really well.

As it turned out, I survived the presentation. Later, when I read through the email comments I received from my classmates (we all had to send in feedback to each group regarding its presentation), I felt a huge sense of relief. The responses blew me away. One said he hadn't been to church in forever but that the presentation made him want to go the following weekend. Another said she believed in the cause and wanted to help out. On and on the positive feedback went, and my heart stirred with each review. (Okay, there was one dissenter who wrote, "Religion is personal. Mind your own business, you bigot." But hey, one out of twenty ain't bad. Plus, there's that verse that says to "count yourselves blessed every time people put you down or throw you out or speak lies about you to discredit me."[1] So, evidently, now I was blessed.)

On the heels of that presentation, I took that proposal, titled "Pulse," to the campus copy shop and told the workers to print as many copies as twenty bucks would buy, the amount of money I happened to have on me that day. I gave those copies to all of my friends leading ministries for the three schools in our area and said, "God has laid on my heart this goal for Christ to be at the pulse of our generation. Would you read this and pray about it? And then let's talk."

From there, word spread. Students came up to me, "Nick, this is so exciting!" or, "Nick, God's totally up to something here!" or, "Wow, Nick, your proposal is awesome, but your graphics? *No bueno.*"

In my mind, I'd think, *Hey, this was an English paper, not a graphic-design project. Cut me some slack!* But before I could say any of that, one guy said, "I have some ideas. Can I take a run at the design?"

Another student said he was a marketing major and had ideas about how to get a campaign like this one off the ground.

Another had thoughts about how to involve campus ministries.

Another was good at fund-raising.

Another was interested in PR.

What could I lose in letting them at it? Within a month of the presentation, the campus was buzzing. I walked into the student union one day and found a group of kids huddled up, praying. I approached them and said, "What's up?" to which they responded, "Nick! We were just praying about what God is doing around here and about this 'Pulse' thing . . . have you heard about it?" I had to laugh. Yeah! I *had* heard about it.

The guys I'd been praying with week after week and I started mobilizing all sorts of teams toward a goal of hosting a regional event the following spring that would reach as many of the twenty-two thousand college students at the three area colleges as we possibly could. Based on our research, we figured that about one thousand of those kids were involved in some kind of church or campus ministry. If every one of those students reached one person for Jesus that year, the impact would only yield two thousand of the twenty-two. Plus, the stats told us that only 10 percent of Christians of any age share their faith. We were staring at a giant math problem. We needed not simple addition but radical multiplication—hence, the need for a big effort, some Mountain Dew, and a whole lot of prayer.

We prayed, and God moved. We began praying for God to show us those who were already living for Jesus and where the greatest concentration of those students existed. Were they premed students? Interior design students? Involved in Greek life? Basketball players? We leaned in as God led, and then we made a beeline for those particular kids and their departments. We needed their help in pulling off something that had never been done in our lifetime—students leading other students en masse to the foot of the cross.

Those early adopters became the first leaders for our prayer groups, which we held every day of the week. When we saw that some students couldn't make the morning prayer times, we launched another seven groups in the evenings. We'd walk up to kids on campus and ask them if they were involved in a prayer group yet, and if they said they couldn't make any of the times when groups were meeting, we'd say, "Well, when can you come?" If they said, "The only time I'm free is Wednesdays from one until two," then we'd say, "We just started a prayer group during that slot! See you Wednesday at one o'clock."

Then we'd run off to go find a leader for the prayer meeting we just launched.

Once we'd rallied a fair number of supporters, all of whom were praying toward the same end, we launched the "G300 Initiative," based on the story of Gideon from the Bible. Gideon was a mighty warrior as well as a devoted follower of God. He wanted to defend his town for God and rallied twenty-two thousand men to his side toward that aim. But God was not pleased. "It's too many men!" God told Gideon. "They will be tempted to think they won the war by their own strength!" God told Gideon to cut his crew.

Gideon trimmed his troops down to ten thousand fighters, but still God said no. "Keep going," God told him. "Your army is still way too fat." This back-and-forth went on, until Gideon had only three hundred men at his side. "Now," God told him, "now we're talking, my friend."[2]

Gideon and his three hundred fighters went on to win the war, and everyone everywhere knew the victory belonged to the Lord. We wanted this same glory for God, and so we called on three hundred people to help. "We all do crazy things to get money for coffee or clothes or dates," I explained, "but have we really sacrificed for God?" I asked three hundred students to each donate one hundred dollars toward reaching their friends for Jesus. "We can each take our money and go do something noble with it," I said, "but if we all put our money on the same table, we can make some noise."

Over the following three months, we raised thirty-three thousand dollars plus change. This dream was getting real.

That fall—September and October of 2005—we hosted a vision event, where those three hundred students rallied and said, "Yeah, we're in. Let's go for it." Next, we held a kickoff event where PULSE was officially launched. Twelve hundred students gathered for that kickoff. From there, we went into high gear toward our big springtime event, and by the time the dust had settled, we had seen eight thousand students encounter Jesus and twelve hundred surrender their lives to him.

And while those big numbers are mind-blowing to look back on, the best part of the experience was seeing our friends and classmates waking up to the reality of Jesus. Around this time, country singer Carrie Underwood exploded onto the national scene with her single, "Jesus, Take the Wheel." It seemed that God was moving everywhere we looked. The whole "Jesus, take the wheel" idea? That's powerful theology. In essence, this is what our friends were saying: "Somebody, please help me stay out of the ditch."

Of course, Jesus would do that and so much more. But we all have to start somewhere—and for many of my peers, that somewhere was the ditch. The message my friends and I were compelled to share back then is the same one I share with you: Jesus is offering you a reset, a do-over, regardless of where you are right now. You could be in the lowest valley, or you could be scraping the sky from a mountainous high. Wherever you are, Jesus is ready to take you farther and deeper. Whether your mistakes are weighty or seemingly insignificant, he says, "Come on. Come with me. I am exactly what you are searching for. Join me as I change the world." Jesus wants to free you and me both from safe and small expectations. He wants to set us free to live out our full potential so that we can know "life that is truly life" (1 Timothy 6:19, NIV).

We watched Jesus do that time and again, never once getting tired of seeing him change a hell-bent life. The students we reached in those early days were longing for the high, the love, the significance, the purpose, the "So what?" of this earthly life. They would meet Jesus and realize that in him, those needs were met. Jesus would prove to be the pinnacle of everything they'd ever known. He would prove to them that the more they knew him, the more they would want to know him. He would prove to them that the more they allowed him to reset their lives, the more they would love their freshly reset life. In many ways, our role reminds me of a captain for the Coast Guard, trolling dangerous waters, looking for people whose lives screamed, "Help!"

When people are adrift at sea, bobbing around in concert to the totally unpredictable winds, all they can focus on is survival—no one has fun clinging to life. But when that rescue boat shows up and the people are lifted from those waters, they can breathe easy once again. They can power ahead in a given direction, sure of their ability to override the wind.

The Bible says that a person who refuses to trust God for wisdom and life is like a wave that is tossed to and fro at sea, never able to steady itself, never able to think clearly. "If any of you lacks wisdom," James 1 says, "you should ask God, who gives generously to all without finding fault, and it will be given to you. But when you ask, you must believe and not doubt, because the one who doubts is like a wave of the sea, blown and tossed by the wind. That person should not expect to receive anything from the Lord. Such a person is double-minded and unstable in all they do" (verses 5–8, NIV). If those without God lack wisdom, then those who turn to Jesus are actually anchored in truth and enabled with a newfound purpose. *How many Instagram likes do I have? Was I invited to the party? What grade did I get on the test? Do I have enough money? Am I sick or healthy? Does she like me or not?* When we're living as people who are anchored in Jesus, these concerns and a thousand others lose their punch. We don't define ourselves the same way anymore.

So, you. What does this have to do with you? The message I've been sharing for the last decade hasn't changed a single bit—not because I'm lazy, but because it's eternally the same. When Billy Graham and friends launched Youth for Christ in the 1940s, they had the slogan "Geared to the Times, Anchored to the Rock." The truth that was true then is still true today. Jesus is for you. Jesus loves you. Jesus is ready to pull you from the wind-whipped waves. Whatever aspect of your life is in need of a reset, he says, "I got this. You can trust me there."

In your self-image, accept his reset.

In your purity, accept his reset.

In your relationships, accept his reset.

In your faith, say, "Jesus, I'm in."

If you're hungry for more, as I've always been, then come to the table. Jesus has been cooking, and I promise it's better than whatever excuse for food is in your fridge. Whatever you are facing, these past years have taught me that he can handle it. Jesus is offering a reset. *Jesus*—the One who changes everything.

1

More to Life

Her name was Michelle, and the razor blade she handed me was suspended from a chain of tarnished steel. Hidden from view, it was worn around her neck every day for five years to remind herself she was worthless. She looked sixteen, maybe seventeen years old. Healthy. Stylish. Normal, in the sense that she could have played forward on her school's soccer team. She didn't look like the kind of kid who was struggling in life—certainly not enough to repeatedly harm herself. As she talked, my heart ached for her.

This was six years into PULSE's existence, only a few years into the ministry God handed to me while I was still in college. I had been speaking on university campuses and in any big-city arena or stadium that would have me, and through a series of connections, I was subsequently invited to tour with a group of bands to forty-seven cities around the country as part of Winter Jam, a gathering that drew about ten thousand students, including teenagers, youth groups, and twenty-somethings each night. The format was straightforward. Bands would open the event, and toward the close of the evening I would take the stage and give a message about Jesus. After the talk, those in the crowd would be given the opportunity to respond. Following the invitation, I made a habit of hanging out at the PULSE table, which on the evening I met Michelle was positioned on the stadium's concourse level in an East Coast city. Each night, I would talk with guys and girls who had questions about Jesus, or pray with those who needed prayer, or hand out *Next* books (portions of God's Word that I try to carry with me wherever I go). Mostly, I just listened. The majority of people who approached me following an event wanted nothing more than a safe, open ear from a guy who cared. I'll admit, I do believe in these kids.

"Michelle, I Love You"

My message that night was the same as it is every night, about the hope and life offered by Jesus. I decided some years back that if I'm going to speak, then my words are going to be about Jesus. That night, I shared from 1 John 1 and spoke about the darkness that we fall into, the pull we feel toward sin, and the culture surrounding us that doesn't have our best interests at heart. I explained how we believe we can find fulfillment in things that will never fulfill . . . and about how a reset is available to us through Jesus. If we needed to reset our priorities, I explained to the ten thousand or so people gathered there that night, then Jesus could help us do that. If we needed to reset our faith, he could help us do that too. If it was our purity or our finances or our family situation or our self-concept or our wayward heart—if anything at all needed to be made new in our lives—Jesus stood ready to set that thing right.

Jesus offers a reset to anyone from anywhere, for anything. All we need to do is turn to him.

When Michelle approached me, she was guarded, as though she wasn't thrilled to be talking to me. "I didn't want to be here tonight," she said. "I hate Christians! They've always judged me and been totally rude. But my friends were coming for the bands, and they asked me if I wanted to come. I've always hated God, if there even is a God . . . because if there is a God, he would never love someone like me."

As she talked, I thought about how healthy and functional she seemed on the outside and how that facade didn't at all match her aura of despair. This girl was angry, certainly at God, and on some level at me.

"You got up to speak tonight," she continued, "and I didn't want to listen to anything you had to say. I couldn't have cared less what you were talking about. I knew none of it applied to me."

Michelle then made eye contact for the first time. Was she warming up to me? "But something happened while you were talking," she continued. "I started hearing this voice saying, 'Michelle, I love you . . . Michelle, I love you . . . Michelle, I love you.' "

Her posture changed as she became quiet and leaned in so only I could hear, "Nick, I think . . . I think it may have been God."

At the end of my talk, when I had invited people to stand up in front of their seat if they wanted to reset some part of their life, Michelle had been compelled to rise to her feet. "I prayed the prayer you told us to pray if we wanted to give our lives to Jesus," she said, "and I meant those words, Nick. I want to start looking to him."

Michelle then punched her fist into the air between us, and reflexively I shifted, thinking she might connect a right hook with my face. Moments before, she had been so revved up that it wouldn't have surprised me. Fortunately her fist stopped, and as it hung there clenched and trembling, she said, "I've worn this for the past five years, and every morning when I put it on, it reminds me that I am worthless. But I'm not going to wear it anymore. I don't want to see myself the way the world sees me one minute longer. I want to start seeing myself the way God sees me. Will you take this?"

My mind spun as I grabbed the blade from her hand. Someone actually wore this? So close to a throat that it could slit?

It was a powerful, larger-than-life moment for Michelle—and for me as well. She had encountered the living God and been changed as a result. Skeptics might say that moving from self-hatred to self-love isn't some simple switch you flip—a one-time decision you make. They'd be completely right, and I told Michelle as much. "You're probably not going to wake up tomorrow and want to join the cast of *Glee.* But you've taken an important step, and now God wants to journey with you every day. And I can tell you from firsthand experience that you're never going to regret this new path."

As Michelle's friends mobbed her, hugging her neck and wiping away her tears, she flashed me a smile. The words conveyed in her bright countenance said, "I knew there had to be more to this life. And I finally found it."

Glimpses of Transcendence

That sense that there is more to this life is something we taste and see throughout our lives. One of my earliest glimpses of it happened when I was just a little boy craving time with my dad. From time to time, my dad (Bruce is his name, but I've always called him "Boom") would pack up the family Suburban and shuttle me five hours north, past the Canadian border, to do some walleye fishing, just the two of us. We'd stop at the corner gas station before heading out of town, where he'd indulge my junk-food compulsion, saying with an easy grin, "Don't tell Mom." The pocketknife he gifted me with during one of those trips I still have, and each time I happen upon it, I'm reminded that our fishing trips were never about the fish but about spending time with my hero.

We always stayed in a cheap motel or lodge, but in my memory those sites were five-star resorts, given the undivided attention I enjoyed from my dad. I can't tell you exactly what we talked about during our days on the road, but two decades later I'm still in touch with those feelings of pride and elation and that sensation of being raised up emotionally by someone I admired so much. To this day, I keep notes from Boom on my desk.

And then there was the time when my mom and I were hanging out on the dock of a lake we frequently visited as a family. We were sitting there talking and laughing when the entire lake turned over. For real: *the whole thing flipped end over end.* Evidently it happens twice a year, this process of a lake's surface waters cooling and thus becoming denser, which causes those waters to sink. The sinking effect makes the bottom layer of water literally turn over and become the top. When it happened in front of us, the result was thousands of fish jumping right out of the water, as though all of creation were putting on a show just for us. It was breathtaking. And a little terrifying. We looked at each other with a mirrored expression: "What the heck was that?" As a young fisherman, I remember being so disappointed that I didn't have my net.

Transcendent moment for sure, that indescribable feeling of rising above.

As a teenager, after I had my driver's license, I would drive down long-forsaken country roads, past the "big city" lights of Fargo, to the middle of nowhere, where the stars would light up the sky. Or I'd float out to the middle of the lake on a raft and watch the northern lights paint the sky as shooting stars raced by. That sense of being a small speck of humanity surrounded by an awesome world—it's enough to undo a person with the magnificence of it all.

It wasn't nature alone that sparked the sense of transcendence for me. When I was seven years old, for instance, my uncle somehow arranged for me to sing "Take Me Out to the Ball Game" during the seventh-inning stretch at a Minnesota Twins baseball game, back when center-fielder sensation Kirby Puckett was still king of the roster and the Twins were in the chase for the title. To be part of the energy, the excitement, the expansiveness of a major league game and to sing before forty thousand excited fans . . . it was larger than life, topped only by the opportunity I was given years later to watch Michael Jordan play during his final year with the Washington Wizards.

Then there were those rites of passage—the first time I held a girl's hand, that first kiss, the process of falling in love. At my college's freshman orientation, I walked into the auditorium looking for the sign with the name "Red Hots," the group I'd been assigned to for the first semester. As music blared from surrounding speakers, I grabbed an open seat next to a girl I'd later learn was named Molly. Molly was too polite to tell me that I'd inadvertently taken the seat of her roommate, who was on a quick bathroom break. When said roommate appeared and eased into the chair beside me, a prompting flooded my mind along the lines of *That could be your wife.*

I glanced nonchalantly at Molly's roommate—a gorgeous, sunny-faced brunette—and then in my spirit said back to God, "If that's you, God, I'm good with that plan."

Molly's roommate was Tiffany, now my wife of eight fantastic years. It was a *really* good plan.

Regardless of the specifics, we've all had these moments when reality is suspended and we're lifted above the fray. Our breath is taken away, maybe, or our eyes water at something deeply moving. Our perspective shifts, our stomach turns, we get goose bumps and shake our heads in disbelief, and we're left utterly and astoundingly undone. It's the glance. The smile. The yes when you ask her out. It's climbing the floating mountains in *Avatar.* It's Augustus telling Hazel Grace in *The Fault in Our Stars* that it would be a privilege to have his heart broken by her. It's the lift before the chorus of Coldplay's "Fix You," that melody that makes everyone unite with arms raised high while Chris Martin raises his fist over the masses of raving fans screaming out the lyrics. It's that thing that's hard to define but easy to spot, that thing called transcendence that elicits from us ecstasy and raw emotion. It's that glimpse that reminds us we're all after something more.

"We were meant to live for so much more,"[3] Switchfoot sings, echoing U2's "I Still Haven't Found What I'm Looking For." We know there is something more.

Seeing the Quest for What It Is

I was about to enter my freshman year of college when I realized that the hunger for that certain "rising above reality" that we all share is at its core spiritual. It was as if God opened my eyes and allowed me at last to see that the concerts and movie scenes, the connections and first kisses, the night sky and the lake flipping itself—none of these things were simply random, but rather glimpses into the reality we were made to experience forever. We were created for transcendence. We were born to be part of something bigger than ourselves. We were made to worship. We were made for intimacy. We were hard-wired to live in a state of awe. This all scratches at the idea philosophers and theologians through the ages have described as our "God-shaped hole."

My new reality was accompanied by a simple command. "Tell them," I felt God was saying. "Tell them that behind it all is me, that I created them to know me."

During the next few years, as almost all of my friends hopped around from one major to the next, from one set of interests to the next, from one relationship to the next, I was a heat-seeking missile on the hunt for anyone who didn't know Jesus. Looking back, I can see that God had been building up to this turn of events. When I was only three or four years old, keeping in line with my highly inquisitive nature, I wandered into my mom and dad's bedroom one morning, where my mom was putting on makeup and doing her hair, and asked her where people go when they die. I hadn't started the conversation there, I should tell you. First, I needed to know why my sister, Jennie, giggled so much and liked the color pink, when my little brother would arrive (Mom was pregnant then), if I could stay up late that night, and whether she and Dad would come watch me play once I made the roster for the Minnesota Twins. But then—*then* I wanted to know what happened when people die.

Her answers, as I recall, went something like, "Because she's a girl. A couple of months. No. Absolutely. And . . . (sigh)." It wasn't an exasperated sigh, but more of a "so I guess we're going to have this conversation now" sigh, an acknowledgment that her hopes for getting my sister and me out the door and into the car so Mom could check off her list of errands were now officially and radically dashed.

After the sigh, my patient and loving mother did her level best to explain to me the mysteries of life and death and life after death, in terms a little boy could understand. And as her words joined into sentences and those sentences filled several paragraphs, Jesus came into my heart—right then, right there, real time. Upon hearing my mom's description of it, I knew I needed Jesus, and so that day at my parents' bedside, I knelt down and handed over the plans to my life. And even though I was only a kid, that moment changed my life.

From that day forward, I was so gripped by this new reality that I made a habit of asking almost everyone I met if they knew Jesus. Mom would be having a conversation with some lady at Target, and I'd jump in with, "Do you know the Lord?" My family would be out for dinner, and I'd pester our server with the same innocent question. By the time I was eleven, I was mailing handwritten letters to Michael Jordan and other national figures I admired in an effort to gauge their spiritual temperature too. I was hunting for some old paperwork recently and found a copy my mom had saved of one of those notes. My grammar and spelling may have left a little to be desired, but the motivation behind the words was pure. It read,

Dear Michael Jordan,

I am writing to you because you are my favorite basketball player. My name is Nick Hall and I think you are the best basketball player in the world. I like you so much that sometimes people I know complain about me talking about you to much! I have a lot of your posters and with my money I bought your rookie card in Fleer. I have 37 of your

> cards in basketball. I have a question for you are you a Christian and do you believe that Jesus died on the cross for everyone who asks him into there life. Well, I hope you are a Christian then I will be able to see you in heaven someday. I hope you get the MVP again this year and I hope the Bulls win another championship.
>
> Your best fan,
>
> Nick Hall

That one was from February of 1993, the year the Bulls rounded out the first of their two three-peats. I'm not sure if MJ ever received my letters or if he has ever surrendered his heart to God, but if not, it wasn't for lack of effort on my part.

During those same years, whenever my buddies and I were playing sports and riding our bikes around the neighborhood, I'd look for every opportunity to ask them questions like, "If you take a hit on the football field and die, do you know where you are going after that?" and, "If you get flattened while you're riding your bike by a car barreling down the street, are you sure you'll go to heaven when you die?" With openers like that, I wasn't exactly the life of the party. But nobody could fault me on the grounds of timidity; I wanted everyone I knew to have a personal relationship with Jesus.

It wasn't until I reached middle school that I realized my do-you-know-Jesus approach wasn't normal . . . or cool. I tried to ease up for a while and learn to talk about other things. But by ninth grade there was such a stirring in my heart that I had to start speaking up again. My youth pastor invited me to attend a national youth conference in Fort Collins, Colorado, where five thousand or so other kids would gather. During one of our days together, we could choose between participating in a community-service project—helping out at a nursing home, I think it was—or else we could go door-to-door in the neighborhood and share Jesus with anything that blinked.

Out of the five thousand conference attendees, approximately 4,950 kids went to the nursing home, while the remaining fifty took to the streets. I was one of the fifty, and after four hours of knocking on doors, sharing how Jesus had changed my life, and praying with complete strangers, I was flying like a kite. I look back now and see how God was preparing me for all that was to come. We may not see his preparation for what it is at the time, but with God, nothing happens by chance.

Years later I was given a partial scholarship to play basketball at Northwestern in Saint Paul, Minnesota, the fulfillment of a lifelong sports dream I'd had. As a (relatively short) kid, I prayed every morning and night that I'd be tall enough to play in the NBA someday, despite the genetic cards I'd been dealt. My prayer went something like, "God I need a miracle! Help me be over six feet tall." My dad is five feet nine inches, and Mom topped out at five foot two, but I'd read somewhere that hanging from monkey bars could stretch a person and make him taller, in addition to eating spinach and guzzling whole milk. Maybe there was hope for me beyond my five-eight stature. I was determined to find out.

On campus my freshman year, I began to experience internal stirrings and sleepless nights (and not solely due to all the ramen noodles and Easy Mac). Beyond my "freshman fifteen" weight fluctuation, God was up to something in my heart in a way I'd never experienced before. I would wake in the middle of the night, crying out for explanations. But typically, aside from the Latin-sounding gibberish my sleep-talking roommate, Derrick, would be muttering, there was only radio silence in return. I needed more input than that.

Many nights, I'd drag myself out of bed and head to the small chapel on campus to plead with God without waking my roommates. "I want to know you," I prayed, over and over again. "I want your cross to mean something to me."

In the midst of those sleepless, prayer-filled nights, God began to soften my heart and open my eyes to his radical love and unconditional grace. My life was divided between my plans and his, my dreams and his. Was I willing to surrender? Pride, lust, a porn habit I battled during high school, and more—there was a lot of normal teenage junk in my life that God was asking me to lay down so that he could raise up in me something new. I remember being terrified to give God the all-access pass, but deep down I knew he was calling me to be all-in and that he was better than anything I was clinging to.

Saying Yes to God

Somewhere along the way, I'd been told that people who were serious about hearing from God fasted and prayed. People in the Bible, ancient monks and desert fathers, serious pastors—they all fasted and prayed. I figured if it was good enough for them, then it was good enough for me. I'd done the praying thing hundreds of times, but fasting was a new frontier—unless legitimate fasting hours were getting racked up while I slept. Still, desperate times call for desperate measures—and I desperately needed to hear from God. I decided to give it a try. That was on a Thursday, during the early days of my freshman year. Basketball season was to start on the following Monday, which meant I was giving God four days to do some explaining as it related to my purpose in life. For those four days I would ingest only water—water, and hopefully a word from the Lord.

A few hours into my debut fast, I was pretty sure I was going to die. I was starving. They say the human body can make it three weeks or longer without food, but in my limited experience, they are wrong. Within three hours, I was reevaluating my strategy and petitioning all of heaven for a quicker response while simultaneously questioning whether the Cheetos fragments on the floor of my car could somehow be my manna from heaven.

That weekend I wound up going back home to Fargo, where I found myself at my old high school for a basketball game. As soon as I entered the gym, I regretted the trip. Popcorn is my kryptonite, and high school sports popcorn holds a special place in my heart (and stomach). As I tried to move quickly through the lobby, I ran into a guy I'd met before named Alan, who was now a freshman at a state school in town. Neither of us had a real reason to be at that game, but the conversation we ended up having proved to be a divine appointment for me.

As we talked about school and our eventual plans, the topic of faith came up. Alan shared that he'd been judged by the church before and had some serious questions. He was feeling what most of us feel when it comes to God: confused. And he didn't know where to turn. There in the lobby of the school gym—right beside the popcorn stand, of course—I kept saying to Alan, "God loves you so much, and he has a huge plan for your life" . . . "God loves you, Alan" . . . "God can handle your dreams and questions" . . . "Jesus is *crazy* about you, Alan."

In the midst of my encouraging Alan, I heard myself interject, "I'm not going to play basketball this year." The words came out of my mouth and were jolting to both Alan and me. Alan met my eyes and said, "Huh?" to which I said, "Huh?" in return. And yet somehow I knew exactly what had transpired. Alan asked, "What are you talking about, Nick? Aren't you on scholarship to play?" I told him that I had been fasting and praying, asking God for direction for my life. And that right there, right in that moment, God had given me the answer I sought.

"I'm supposed to devote my life—all of it—to sharing Jesus," I told Alan with a grin. "I'm not going to play basketball this year. Why would I spend all that time and energy on hoops when the whole reason I'm here is to tell people about Jesus?" I laughed then, the sort of relieved chuckle that reflexively surfaces when you realize you finally found what you'd been looking for.

On the heels of that exchange with Alan, I had a whole slew of questions for God. What did all of this mean? Where was I supposed to go? And once I got to wherever I was going, what was I supposed to do once I arrived? I wasn't trying to be the next Billy Graham or anything—although I would go on to read his biography four consecutive times. I just wanted to do what God had asked me to do. I would sit with those questions day after day, even as a phrase kept returning to my mind, something of a motto for my place in the world: "My life exists to put Christ at the pulse of a generation." I would plaster it on my notebooks, on the screen saver of my laptop, and, most importantly, on my living, beating heart. *Christ at the pulse* and nothing else. I would shorten the phrase further to the single word *pulse,* and in one fell swoop a pasty-white kid from North Dakota would be the possessor of a divinely captivating dream. Pulse . . . my commitment and passion. Pulse . . . my ministry and goal. Pulse . . . my hope for a generation. Pulse . . . God's call on my life.

Two years later—in 2004—I would write the paper detailing the dream for how to reach my generation with the message of Jesus' love. That paper would gain some recognition, spawning a campus-wide, student-led initiative to reach every college student in our city. Within five years, more than fifty thousand students would be impacted with that message, and more than ten thousand of them would respond positively to the gospel, making it one of the largest student-led evangelism movements in all of United States history. A few months later, PULSE opened a national office in Minneapolis, Minnesota, in order to take the message of hope and redemption coast to coast . . . and well beyond.

But before all of that: *popcorn*. Now that God had spoken to me there in that gym, I could finally break my fast.

2

Don't Settle

When I first started PULSE, a handful of trusted friends agreed to dive into running it with me—among them my best friend, Troy, who was working at a Pepsi bottling plant at the time. "Troy, will you quit your job and join me?" I asked him. "Let's go after this thing and see what God does." We would meet together frequently with a few others to pray about the ministry—what we were trying to accomplish, how we planned to accomplish it, who we wanted to serve, and so forth. We really had no clue what we were doing, so those prayer times were vital to us. We needed wisdom. Direction. Some sort of divine intervention to save us from ourselves.

During those prayer meetings at the Cornerstone Coffee House next to the homeless shelter in downtown Fargo, we'd talk about what we were seeing in our friends and classmates, about the problems we knew only Jesus could solve. If I were to nail down the single greatest recurring theme for those prayers, it was how on earth a generation with so much potential could also be in so much pain. This is a generation—often referred to as Millennials—that is filled to overflowing with energy and passion and compassion. We saw in our peers the insatiable desire to give themselves to something worthwhile, something of substance, something that would last. We saw gifts and abilities, talent like you can't believe, and a spirit of immortality, which helps them say yes to the risks that nobody else wants to take. This generation doesn't see race, color, creed, or religion. They simply see people. They love people. They hate systems of injustice, hypocrisy, conformity, and for the most part, they even hate *hate.* What's more, they're pretty good with technology.

And yet it was within this same circle of people that rampant brokenness, deviance, drug abuse, angst, gang affiliation, suicide, eating disorders, and self-harm were taking hold. One of our peers hanged himself inside his fraternity's house, and another became so intoxicated that she fell into the river and drowned. Still today, the issues my buddies and I saw more than ten years ago continue to haunt my generation:

- The average undergrad is drunk for 10.6 hours a week.[4]
- 81 percent of teens have the opportunity to use illicit drugs; 42.5 percent try them.[5]
- Ninety-three percent of boys and 62 percent of girls are exposed to Internet porn before the age of 18.[6]
- Fifty-nine percent of young Christians disconnect from their church, either permanently or for an extended time, after the age of 15.[7]
- Suicide is the third leading cause of death for youth ages 10 to 24.[8]
- Twenty-five percent of adolescents have an episode of major depression during high school, with the average age of onset being 14 years.[9]

It was baffling to us all. So much promise, and yet pain on every side. More than anything, we wanted to help.

Giving the World's Way a Try

It's worth calling into question what culture says about real life. What are the messages being sent our way about where to find hope, meaning, and how to thrive in this world? Writing this, I just clicked on Spotify's Global Top 50.[10] I wish you were here for this dance party.

From the Weeknd: "Drugs started feelin' like it's decaf . . . and all these mother—— want a relapse."[11]

From Fetty Wap: "No one can control us, ay, yeaaaah baby."[12]

From Drake: "I know when that hotline bling, it can only mean one thing."[13]

From OMI: "I think that I found myself a cheerleader. . . . She grants my wishes like a genie in a bottle."[14]

From Macklemore: "Got gas in the tank, cash in the bank, and a bad little mama with her a—— in my face."[15]

Lady Gaga says being "beautiful and dirty rich"[16] is the ticket. Ke$ha says the answer is cash, beer, and men who "look like Mick Jagger."[17] TLC says the answer to life's questions is found in doing it all night[18] and losing control. For Far East Movement, it's drinking until you get "slizzard" and "fly like a G6"[19] (the plane, not the Pontiac, I think). Avril Lavigne says the key is ditching the good-girl ways and adopting a "what the hell"[20] attitude toward life. John Mayer says it's to get high, call a girl from your past, and "fake love for an hour."[21] And for Katy Perry, it's dancing until you die, getting drunk, and going "all the way tonight."[22]

Now, I want to be clear of my intent here. I'm not listing these lyrics in order to pass judgment. I actually like a lot of the music I just listed—in moderation, anyway. But I think we need to question the message we are lifting up and what we are allowing to enter our hearts and minds. If you listen to a message long enough, you will start to reflect its content.

If you were to list the themes of today's most popular music, television shows, movies, and games, you'd wind up with some pretty powerful messages—like "This moment is all that matters." And "Pleasure will fill any void." And how about this one: "'Likes' determine your worth." Or this: "Get all you can while you can." It's pretty straightforward, right? And all around us are people doing exactly what the world says will satisfy.

We climb into the friend's car and recklessly peel in and out of traffic while posting Instagram videos. The moment is all there is, and we don't really care what unfolds.

We throw back a few shots and light up with our buddies, get a little slizzard—all good.

We say yes to that coworker we've been interested in because hooking up is where it's at.

We drink. And drug. And party. And chase money. And have sex—which is oh so special until we get diseases—because this is what life is about. There's the high, the jolt, and something freeing, and something powerful, and because the moment is all that matters, we're determined to make that moment count.

For a season, those moments are fun. This is something they don't typically tell you in church, by the way: sin is fun. *Really* fun. When I was growing up, the general position held by most churches was that kids not living for God were to be pitied. They were "lost and miserable" and going nowhere fast. "They're really missing out," youth leaders would tell us. "They're so empty and so in pain."

By the time I started college, I heard my fair share of stories from people who were lost but now found, falling right in line with the claims asserted by the famous old hymn "Amazing Grace." They were blind to the things of God but were at last able to see. While I listened to their testimonies at varying church meetings, I remember thinking my story was lame.

The testimonies came from frat boys who had made a sport out of beer pong and ladies, or the guy who survived a string of wild nights courtesy of his addictions to blackjack and bongs, or the businessmen who had indulged in private jets, nightclubs, shopping sprees, excessive drinking, and elaborate vacations on their way to the top. There were women who shared too, but the stories that stuck with me most as a young dude were those of men who were remorseful but also sounded like they had a lot of fun. Was I supposed to feel sorry for them or envious of them? I don't think jealousy was what our pastor had in mind.

In the same way that those men never called their checkered past "fun," I never felt liberty to tell anyone I was jealous of those pre-Jesus themes. I was a normal, impressionable kid trying to make my way toward being a man, and each time I'd hear someone deliver a radical testimony—"I was drinking and partying and living life in a total haze, until I had this amazing encounter with Jesus, and then he turned everything around for good!"—I'd think, "Why can't I serve Jesus a little later in life, after I've had my share of good times too?" We used to jokingly call it taking time to build our testimony.

I wasn't mature enough to realize that those seemingly awesome moments always came to a not-awesome end, and there are few emotions stronger than regret. The party ended, the buzz fizzled, the high faded, the money ran out, the hookup unhooked herself, reality evicted the fantasy, and the car eventually flipped. When you live like there are no consequences, the consequences come crashing in. It all turns ugly in the end.

Where Satisfaction Isn't Found

A few weeks ago, Tiffany and I took our three-year-old son, Truett, down the street to a neighborhood pool to play. There is a splash pad there that Truett loves, but he is always a little nervous about doing it alone. The fountains are unpredictable, and while he thinks getting soaked is fantastic, he craves a little more control over the timing of it all. As soon as we arrived, he started in on his "Daddy, come, Daddy, come!" spiel, and so I raced over to the pad and started chasing him around. There were three thick metal arches that also sprayed water, one about five feet tall, one six feet tall, and one seven feet tall. They fanned out and increased in height as you went—first the small one, then the medium one, then the tall. Truett and I fell into a routine of running in circles through all of the arches, dashing in and out of them probably fifteen times in a row. We were laughing hard by the last round, which is probably why I lost focus and ran right into the shortest arch. I took the turn too fast, my foot slipped on the wet surface, and *bam,* I nailed my head.

Lying on the ground completely dazed, I reflexively reached for my head—first, to make sure it was still attached to the rest of my body, and second, to see if there was any blood. As it turned out, there was blood. A lot of blood. My wife is a certified physician's assistant, which is why I trusted her assessment that although I'd suffered a serious blow, I didn't need stitches, a visit to the hospital, or a funeral (I can be dramatic). I was going to live, she said.

We headed back home after that, and in the ensuing days I got some good laughs showing friends and family the video Tiffany happened to be shooting of Truett and me when I had my personal *America's Funniest Home Videos* moment. (Search #resetmyheadinjury on Instagram for proof.)

I look at that footage now and think, *I wonder if that's how it happens with sin. We're cruising along in life—awesome, awesome, awesome, awesome! And then all of a sudden,* bam! As we lie there, writhing in pain, we think, "Two minutes ago, I was having so much fun."

In January 2000, VH1 put out a list of its top one hundred rock-and-roll songs of the millennium. Not merely a "best of" ten-year or hundred-year list, but a list covering a full thousand years. (Never mind that rock-and-roll didn't exist before the 1940s.) The number-one song, beating out the Beatles, the Eagles, the Doors, and the Who, was the Rolling Stones' "(I Can't Get No) Satisfaction." Admittedly, song lyrics were a little . . . um, simpler . . . in 1965, when this particular song was written. But still, you can't help but notice in the refrain a strain, a deep-seated ache.

"I can't get no satisfaction," it says. "'Cause I try . . ."[23]

And we try.

And we try.

And we try.

And we try.

And *still,* satisfaction can't be found.

If you're alive and kicking, you relate to this ache. I do too. We have all tried, and tried, and come up empty in the end.

I caught an interview a few years ago with New England Patriots quarterback Tom Brady. This dude is the Great American Hero. He has Super Bowl trophies and is married to one of the world's most popular supermodels. At the time of the interview he had already won three NFL championships and yet candidly said he still thought there was something greater out there for him. "I mean, maybe a lot of people would say, 'Hey man, this is what is.' I reached my goal, my dream, my life. I think, 'God, it's got to be more than this.' I mean, this can't be what it's all cracked up to be."

Steve Kroft, the interviewer, looked at Brady and said, "What's the answer?" to which he answered, "I wish I knew. I wish I knew. . . . I love playing football and I love being quarterback for this team, but, at the same time, I think there's a lot of other parts about me that I'm trying to find."[24]

In *Parade* magazine sometime later, I saw a print interview with a reflective Shia LeBeouf, one of my favorite actors, in which he acknowledged his frailty and fear. "Actors live dependent on being validated by other people's opinions," he told the interviewer. "I don't understand what it is I do that people want. I don't know what an actor does. I have no credentials. I don't know what I'm doing. . . . Acting is instinctual. The good actors are all screwed up. They're all in pain. It's a profession of bottom-feeders and heartbroken people."

Later, when the interviewer asked LeBeouf why he and his love interest hadn't made it, Shia said, "Man, I have no idea. What was that all about? I have no answers to anything. None. Why am I an alcoholic? I haven't a [expletive] clue! What is life about? I don't know."[25]

Brady and LeBeouf aren't the only ones who have searched in the wrong places for the answer to what will satisfy. Everyone tries and tries . . . and tries some more. I meet middle-aged men on their third or fourth marriage, still insisting that the answer is another fling. And binge drinkers insisting the answer is another night out with friends. And a thousand other people of every age and background, still insisting that the answer is more speed, more frequency, more hits, more highs, more hookups, more likes, more of whatever they're hoping is filling the void that is too painful to admit they have. If they can just keep filling their lives full of distraction, they won't have to face the fact that they're dying inside.

Even so, they are dying inside. Without something to live for, we all are dying inside.

Flip Side of the Fantasy

This is why there are just as many songs written about the emptiness that we experience after following the path the party songs so brazenly paved. Linkin Park sings, "All I wanna do is trade this life for something new."[26] Three Days Grace sings, "I need a change and I need it fast; I know that any day could be the last."[27] And then there's Bruno Mars: "I would die for you, baby, but you won't do the same."[28] The list goes on and on. Behind the catchy beats and cool rhythms is a universal, paralyzing pain. We know the pain all too well. The thing we thought would make us happy didn't work, and now we've got a dilemma on our hands. How are we supposed to patch the gaping hole this terrible pain has left behind?

Long after the crowd had dispersed, on that night when Michelle handed me the razor blade, I spent some time alone in the stands, thinking about how she'd sunk to such desperate depths. Here was a girl who had youth, beauty, vibrancy, and potential on her side. She had friends. A family. People who wanted to see her succeed. And yet somewhere along the way she decided to thread that razor blade on a chain and clasp that chain around her neck. Day after day, she would unhook that chain and drag the blade across her arms and legs until her blood bubbled up and flowed, thin streams of self-hatred, self-disgust. She'd then clean the blade, rethread it through the chain, hook the chain around her neck, tuck the blade underneath her clothes, and move through her day in a state of numb despair, wishing for an escape hatch from this life.

The night after I met Michelle, I was speaking in the next city up the coast, and partway through my talk, I told the crowd about the conversation she and I'd had. As I explained what had happened with Michelle—her despair, her salvation, her new life—I (very carefully) pulled her razor blade and chain from my jacket pocket and held it up for the thousands gathered to see. And then I told them that regardless of what their darkness looked like, it too could be brought into the light. There was nothing too dark and too far gone for Jesus to reset.

From there, Michelle's story went viral, and my team and I began to notice that those coming to later tour dates were entering the arenas with tangible evidence of their darkness and pain. We began setting out huge aluminum garbage cans we called "reset bins," in order to collect the contraband. And toward the end of each evening's event, I'd invite anyone who needed a reset in any aspect of life to come forward and either place their gear in the bins or write on a card what was tripping them up so that they could symbolically throw it away.

Each night I would stand by one of those bins, and I will never forget those moments as hundreds of students walked by me, tossing in their stuff. Knives, flasks, game controllers, pornographic magazines, iPods, bullets, miniature whiskey bottles, lighters, drug paraphernalia, condoms, cut-up credit cards, bottles of pills—icons of fun that wound up not being able to deliver on their promise. The items many carried and the stories so many told were shocking; but still, light was breaking in. In the midst of godless situations, God was moving.

Following the events, a percentage of those same people would approach me to talk about what they'd ditched and why it mattered to them. What struck me throughout those conversations was not how deviant or rebellious they were, but rather how these were normal kids trying to be happy, even as happiness refused to be had.

Bono isn't the only one who still hasn't found what he's looking for[29]; we've all searched in vain for that magic high, and we've all come up short in the end. And night after night on that tour, I stared at scores of bins overflowing with contraband reflecting our coping mechanisms of choice. The needles, the pill bottles, the booze, the porn—it was a generation's way of screaming, "Save me from myself. I can't take this anymore."

The truth is we all want to be saved.

3

Good and Also True

The years from 2004 until 2014 were a beautiful blur of activity as I became not only a husband and a father but also more confident than ever that I was exactly where God wanted me to be in life, doing exactly what he'd asked me to do. All through the Bible there is a pattern of God taking ordinary people and accomplishing extraordinary things in and through their lives, and this was certainly the case with me. I was nineteen years old when he invited me onto the wild ride known as PULSE, and the combination of my youth, my inexperience, and my naiveté about the ways of the global ministry world almost immediately prompted wiser, more established, more successful ministry leaders to take me under their wings. They've never said as much, but I suspect they just pitied me and didn't want me to get crushed. Either way, throughout those early years, I was given opportunities that up-and-coming communicators would give a right arm for. I traveled. I spoke. I asked questions of my heroes. I grew. That early exposure catapulted PULSE in a way I didn't earn or deserve. God was at work, blowing me away at every turn.

By now I was convinced that God was asking me to carry his message of forgiveness, grace, and love to the entire nation I call home. As a ministry, we'd already done events in thirty-nine of the fifty states, reaching two and a half million people and seeing a half million of them respond to the gospel. But in my heart, I knew God was calling us to dig deeper. This was never about PULSE or anything I could do on my own. "Gather my people together," the whisper went, "as many as will come, all in one place, and tell them they're loved by me. Tell them I'm offering a reset today." Everywhere I looked I saw division and brokenness—in individual lives, in families, in schools and neighborhoods, in our country at large. This event would prove to us all that unity exists, that wholeness is available, and that we can leverage their power for good.

I shared my vision for a nationwide gathering—my instincts told me the best place to hold it would be on the National Mall in Washington, DC—with Tiffany and a handful of leaders at PULSE. The idea consumed us so much that we restructured our whole organization around it. We were captivated by the idea of an effort so large that no one could take credit for it but God himself. We spent months planning and strategizing, praying and brainstorming, racking our minds for the most effective way to sound the alarm, to let everyone know that regardless of what their life had looked like in the past, Jesus was offering them a reset today.

During one of those sessions, somebody had the idea of doing a road trip across America, stopping in a different locale each day in order to invite people to DC. We were eyeing July of 2015 for our event but quickly realized that based on the scale and sheer logistics involved in pulling off such a massive undertaking, we'd better push it to 2016. We'd call the experience "Together 2016," and we'd pray for a million people to come. Now, we needed an RV.

The Day the Jesus Mobile Broke Down

Despite the fact that I'd never ridden in a recreational vehicle, let alone driven one, when a generous businessman who had learned of our road-show aspirations offered to give PULSE his RV, I couldn't say yes fast enough. My friends and I had the thing wrapped in a giant not-so-subtle yellow sticker that read "The Largest Jesus Gathering in American History" and headed off for our first stop. Before it was all said and done, we would hit thirty cities in six weeks, from Las Vegas to Phoenix to San Diego, up to LA, Sacramento, and Seattle, over to Denver, Minneapolis, Chicago, and New York, down to Orlando and back over to Dallas and more. We would spread our message in churches and on college campuses, in arenas and in stadiums—anywhere those cities would have us, we would show up with passion and speak.

The bands traveling with us were a draw for those gatherings but also added a thick layer of complexity to the whole deal. Essentially, we would pull into a town, spend the day setting up, do our event that night, spend hours tearing down, load everything back into our RV-led caravan, and drive through the night to the next town. The travel and task list would have been enough on its own, but to make things more interesting, we did the majority of the thirty-stop trip with two infants in tow. Truett was a baby then, and the couple that Tiffany and I were traveling with also brought their months-old child. After hundreds of freshly filled diapers and more than enough sweaty clothes, the RV was less than glorious.

To maintain sanity, each of the six adults on board would take turns driving while the other five caught some z's. One night in particular I was awakened by the distinct smell of smoke. There had been myriad odors along the way, but this was a new one. As I wiped sleep from my eyes and tried to sort out what city and state we were in, I noticed that we were pulled over on the side of the highway, and that the smoke was coming from *our* engine. It seemed theologically impossible that the Jesus Mobile could break down, and yet there we were, stalled and sad. This was going to be a very long day.

As the story unfolded, I learned that the driver, who shall remain nameless, had pulled over to get gas a few hours prior and in deference to our shoestring budget (or massive sleep deprivation) had selected the cheapest fuel grade available. All of this would have been great, except that the cheapest gas was unleaded, something a diesel engine generally doesn't like.

Three hours and several thousand dollars later, the Jesus Mobile had been towed into Saint Louis to have its stomach unceremoniously pumped and we were depressingly broke as we sped away to make it to the night's event.

On Siphoning and Salvation

It didn't occur to me at the time—I was too discouraged, exhausted, and annoyed to see it then—but later, upon further reflection, I saw that roadside breakdown as a perfect metaphor for our cause. The reason we were in the Jesus Mobile was that we were committed to gathering people together. And the reason we wanted to gather people together was to tell them about Jesus' overwhelming love. And the reason we wanted to tell people about Jesus' love was that we knew they were tired of trying, trying, trying, trying to find satisfaction, only to be let down. The sole thing that could possibly satisfy them was the love of Jesus! We knew this to be true and deeply wanted to spread the word.

It was as if an entire generation of teens and twenty-somethings was funneling unleaded gas into lives that were created to run on diesel and facing major costs as a result. "You were created for more," I would declare each night. In the same way that the RV expert was the only one who could diagnose our problem there in Saint Louis and then help us sort out a plan for getting our vehicle back on the road, only Jesus—the one who oversaw the creation of our soul's system—could determine all that was lacking and provide what we needed in order to thrive.

Jesus says that he came to give us life to the full (see John 10:10). He stands at the door to our lives and knocks, and if any of us will hear his voice and open the door, he will come and share a meal with us "together as friends" (Revelation 3:20, NLT). I love that last part—sharing a meal with the living God, together as friends. When the RV mechanic siphoned out the bad gas so that he could refill the tank with proper fuel, it was a mess of plastic tubing, gurgled pumping, and exasperated sighs. But not so with Jesus. He simply invites us to come to him. And his invitation is so welcoming that it's equated to the casualness of home, companionship, and food. My kind of guy, for sure.

One of my favorite things in life is sharing a meal with close friends. There's something so disarming about breaking bread around a table. Growing up, we had a big island in our kitchen where family and friends would gather. We would feast on the food my dad was dishing up and laugh at the stories told by my crazy, awesome mom. My memories from that kitchen are so rich—so much laughter, so much food, so many cans of Coke, so many real conversations. Gathering together in that way always invited transparency and openness. If someone was struggling, we would carry the burden together. If someone needed prayer, we would come together and lift our voices to heaven. And if someone simply needed one of Mom's famous cookie bars, there were always plenty to go around (assuming you got there early).

To those of us who are weary, beat up, and begging for an escape from this life, Jesus says, "No, no, no. You don't need an escape. You just need something that will truly satisfy." He looks at us with all of our waywardness, wounds, and worries and says, "You, there. I want to spend time with you. You don't need to change or be 'good enough' to spend time with me. I love you right now. I believe in you. I believe you can be just like me. I believe you can love like me. Think like me. Talk like me. Act like me. And I won't give up on you until that vision comes to pass."

This sounds crazy, doesn't it? That Jesus would take a broken person who has screwed up time and time again, and ask that person to have dinner with him night after night after night? It seems scandalous. This is the perfect Son of God we're talking about, not some suspicious transient on the streets. As it turns out, we're the suspicious transients on the streets, and to us Jesus says, "Hey! Really good to see you. You doing anything tonight?"

Say yes to his offer, surrender, and then look out. He will come in and never, ever leave. This may sound terrible, sort of like that friend who smells a little funky and always sticks around a little too long. (If you can't think of that friend, it just might be you.) But it's not like that at all. Jesus is the friend you've always wanted. The kind of friend you would do anything for. He lives fully. He listens intentionally. He takes risks and has no fear. He displays a radical love the world doesn't quite know what to do with, and the moment we start hanging out with him—surrendering to him, following him, allowing him to transform us from the inside out—his heart of love and risk and ridiculous compassion starts to form inside us. We start to think differently. And dream differently. And see the world with different eyes.

Unlearning What We've Been Taught

I spend about two hundred days a year talking with people about this exact same message and inviting people to respond. And what the days and years have taught me is that people would have a much easier time accepting this version of the gospel if it looked like anything they'd seen before. For too many of us, the spiritual waters have become so muddied that there has to be a reintroduction to the real Jesus Christ.

For example, I grew up in a place where everyone was a Christian—cultural Christian, that is. We were baptized as infants, confirmed as teenagers, and Christian from that point forward, if we had to check a box on a form. But the designation carried no weight in life beyond an occasional church service and some superficial kindness. It was being Christian the same way someone could be a Green Bay Packers fan. Actually, the investment was even less for their spiritual side, seeing as they'd pay hard-earned money to wear Packers gear.

Cultural Christianity is alive and well today and shows up in plastic church smiles and managed faith, in "being good people" who secretly battle our demons alone, in allowing contention and strife to mark our families, in collecting more toys as we drown in debt.

In the same region where I grew up (and in communities all over the world), there were other Christians whose lives were affected substantively by the designation, but the result was defining their existence by disapproval or fear. These Christians clung so tightly to their list of laws, regulations, and picket signs that the love of Jesus was nowhere to be found. They were like an angry mob, throwing stones at anyone who didn't believe the way they believed and wearing judgment like a badge. Rather than being defined as those who loved our enemies, we were all too easily defined by who our enemies were.

Another message delivered to my friends and me when we were growing up was that a person would have to be ignorant not to believe in God. "Look at the stars!" well-meaning adults would say. "I mean, duh, of course there's a God!"

But then those same buddies and I went off to college and met dozens of friends and professors who were thoughtful, rational, brilliant intellectuals who happened not to believe in Jesus at all. They had tough questions of Christianity—Is this real? Is it true? Does it matter in the end?—questions that sure seemed to warrant a better answer than something like, "Look at the stars, you idiot. Duh."

An entire generation has grown up pretty confused about what being Christian means. We don't want to sign up for being a slacker, someone who says they associate with Jesus but whose life is unchanged. And we have zero desire to be one of the "bigots" who claims to know and love Jesus while despising the very people Jesus came to save. And because we see no third option, we disregard the whole deal and move on. Which is why, as various studies have reported, as soon as Mom and Dad aren't around to force church attendance, older teens and early twenty-somethings quit going, in what I consider a modern-day Exodus—literally millions of Millennials walking away from the church.[30] This also explains why this generation seeks community so readily in the party crowd; at least in those circles what you see is what you get—no hypocrisy, no condemnation.

Actually, there are at least ten things the church could learn from the bar scene, "foster genuine community" being just one. I was sitting in church one Sunday, daydreaming about all the ways the experience (which that particular day was a slow death) could be improved. "If going to church were more like going to a bar," I scribbled in my church bulletin, "then more people would love going to church." Want to see a few of the lessons that made my top ten? Here's one: *Rejoice with people's victories and mourn with people's losses.* We say we do that in the church, but you have to admit the bar scene does it far better.

Or how about this one: *Engage multiple generations.* Why nearly 100 percent of the church experience is segregated by age, I'll never know. Stick some old people with some young people, boldly declare the truths of Scripture, open it up for conversation, and let the sparks fly as they may.

And then there's this: *Have a product that actually delivers on the promises it makes.* While there's no question that God delivers on his promises, unfortunately his Spirit is nowhere to be seen in many places of worship.

Anyway, I digress. My point is that in a world of misplaced trust and rampant corruption, pretense and posturing, church-as-institution and the religious spirit, there stands Jesus—calling, knocking, loving, waiting, eager to come in and break bread. If you are jaded by religion, then look to the one willing to turn over the religious tables in order to capture your heart.[31] When all of the senseless layers we've tried to shroud him in have been stripped back and allowed to fall to the ground, there stands Jesus, in all his glory, friend of the sin-stained heart. He welcomes reject and royalty alike, the religious and the irreligious. Jesus welcomes everyone, and he changes everything.

Jesus—and Nothing More

One of my favorite parts of what I do is being there for students when the lights turn on that Jesus is better than anything they'd imagined or hoped. In the same way that Michelle "hated Christians and hated God," scores of students I talk to have settled on a less-than-favorable opinion of this whole Christianity deal before they've really even given Jesus a chance. Many of them have tried church. They have tried youth groups. They have tried reading the Bible. They have tried saying a prayer from time to time. But they've never tried Jesus—as Messiah, as Savior, as friend. Once they encounter Jesus—not as a religious figurehead or a political candidate or an angry judge ready to exile us to hell, but as a gentle and just shepherd who is committed to abundance and grace—it's like the eye doctor finally getting their prescription right, and for the first time in life they can see.

They see that Jesus is real. He came. He died. He was raised from the grave. And in his sacrifice, we can be made whole. It's totally too good to be true, and yet it is that good and also that true.

They see that he is revolutionary. Despite the lame version of Jesus that has been thrust upon us, Jesus is the opposite of weak and safe. He is a man of great conviction, willing to go to the cross for what he believed. When he was on the scene, everyone knew it. He had all the power, he showed all the love, he reached out to the entire world, and still today we mark time by his life.

They see that he forces a response. You can't encounter Jesus without forming an opinion about who he is. His claims, his teachings, his incarnation, his love—what will you do with this Jesus? What will you say in response?

Someone once said to me, "To some people, Jesus was a great teacher. And he was. There is so much wisdom to be gleaned from him that we'll never fully absorb it all. To some people, Jesus was a great prophet, and that also is true. His words were powerful indeed. And to some people, those whom the Holy

Spirit reveals, Jesus is Messiah. The only question that remains is which one of those people are you?"

Whenever I invite people to take Jesus at his word and declare him the leader of their lives, I can see in their expressions the wrestling match that ensues. They want the acceptance and the abundance that Jesus promises, even as they can't reconcile the seeming lunacy of going God's way. The mental gymnastics are legitimate: it is lunacy to follow God. It always has been too. Think about Noah, Abraham, or scores of others who have followed his call.

"Noah, go build a boat . . . for several decades." (Can you imagine what his in-laws said about him?)

"Abraham, leave everything you know, and I will show you where to go later." (Try fitting that into your five-year master plan.)

"Follow me," Jesus said to the men who would become his disciples, "and I'll show you life as it was meant to be lived." He says the same thing to us today: "Trust me. Follow me. Give it all. Come to me dirty, and I'll clean you up. Come broken, and I'll reassemble the parts. Come desperate, and I'll replace your pain with joy. Come to me with all your questions, all your suspicions, all your confusion, all your fear, and I'll install my Spirit of revelation and wisdom and guidance permanently into your heart."

There are no formulas, magic wands, or fairy dust here; only Jesus, the righteous rebel who saves the world—loveable lunatics included.

A Call to Surrender

Maybe you've heard all of this before, or maybe this is the first time. Maybe you know the claims of Jesus like the back of your hand, or maybe what I'm talking about is earth-shattering news to you. Maybe you've been following him for years, or maybe saying yes would mean that despite all the time you've spent running, today you're coming home. Whatever your background, whatever your assumptions, whatever your circumstances here and now, here's what I want to say to you: You don't have to go one more second in this life without knowing Jesus—his love, his care, his presence, and his joy. He is standing at the door to your heart and calling your name, asking if it's cool to come in. "Michelle, I love you!" he whispered to that young woman, right in the depth of her pain. Your name is on his lips as well. He loves you just the same. Let go of all the secondhand information you've heard about God. Lean into the still, small voice calling your name. Trust that your heavenly Father will never lead you astray. Stake your future on this cause, this man.

A Swiss genius many regarded as the greatest Protestant theologian of the twentieth century, Karl Barth, once was asked about the most profound thought he'd ever learned during his years of research and study. Now, Barth was the one whose greatest known work was a six-million-word, thirteen-volume series explaining the doctrines of God, his Word, his creation, and how humankind gets reconciled to him, a project that took Barth more than three decades to write. Normal people can barely understand *Church Dogmatics,* let alone write it. This guy knew his stuff. And yet in response to that question about the most profound thought he'd ever learned, here is what he said: "Jesus loves me, this I know, for the Bible tells me so."[32]

At the end of the day, it all comes down to the straightforward claims of Jesus and to how we will respond. He knows you. He sees you. He loves you in ways that cannot be replicated or overcome. Now, what are you going to do with that?

In Need of a Reset

I'm kind of an early adopter with technology, in that if the money is available, I love being one of the first to have the newest technology. Many times, I've purchased the newest phone on the day of its release, and once, I even stood in line before the store opened. There's something about opening up a brand-new, cutting-edge piece of technology. Everything looks right, feels right, and works exactly as it should.

The reason we appreciate new things is that we know all too well what it's like to use old ones. Your battery dies in two hours, your apps are a mess, your memory is full, and your phone is sluggish, to say the least. Oh, for those new-phone days!

In the world of technology, one of the greatest inventions has to be the reset button. Click that handy button and your phone or tablet is as good as new. It's like a giant rewind button in the cloud: *Bwwwwwwhup!* All of a sudden, dead links are cleared out, speedy connections resume, and all is right in your technology world. Your system has been reset, back to the device's life as it was meant to be lived.

The offer of a reset is exactly what the gospel is about. Jesus siphons out the junk that has gummed up our system for far too long and pours in pure, clean fuel to propel us down the right path. He resets our systems—our habits and attitudes, our priorities and pursuits—and instills in us the incredible reality that we're living the life we were made for, "real and eternal life," as John 10:10 promises, "more and better life" than we ever dreamed of. As good as that reset smartphone feels, a spiritual reset is second to none. It's like New Year's Day for the soul, the day when there's nothing but a clean, fresh start. And it's available every day.

"What is it for you?" I always ask people. "What part of your life most needs to be reset?" I get all sorts of answers to that question: "My addiction." "My worries over what people think of me." "My cynicism." "My fears." "My habits." "My self-image." "My identity." "My past." There are as many categories in need of spiritual reset as there are people on the planet, I suppose. But my guess is that for you, in your specific life, there is one big thing that above all other facets of life is causing you undue confusion and pain. There is probably one thing that, were it reset back to God's original design, would yield the greatest sense of relief for you. Most people I know are closely acquainted with the failures, foibles, and sin in their life. They know what the one thing is.

It's self-harm.

Or manipulation.

Or substance abuse.

Or pride.

It's overworking.

Or overspending.

Or performing to gain self-worth.

It's sexual promiscuity.

Or an apathetic attitude.

It's rage.

Whatever has been tripping you up, a reset is available to you. You don't have to earn it, buy it, beg for it, or swipe it when nobody's looking. It is yours, free of charge. It is yours, by the grace of God. All you have to do is receive it, open hands and open heart. Say yes to the life you were meant to live. Say yes to a Father who's good.

Across the next eight chapters, we'll look at some ways to get that done.

PART II

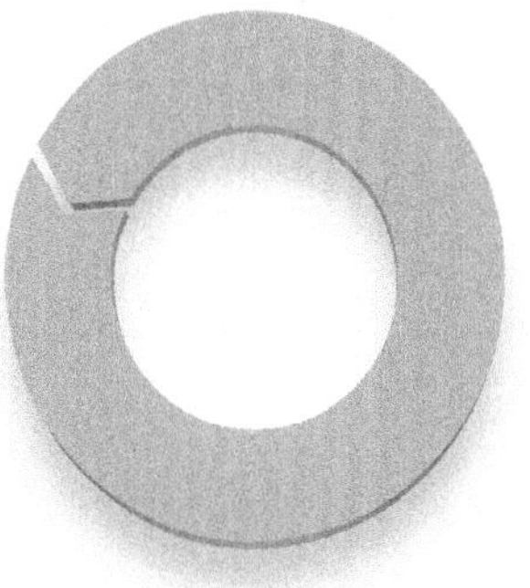

Hitting Reset

Ready to Change

In part 1, I explained how God has captured my heart for the message of Jesus, and while I'm serious about my commitment to him, even those of us who love God are drawn to rebel against him from time to time and go our own way instead. The same brokenness that was in Adam and Eve lives in all of us, and every time we look to the world to fill our void we turn our backs on the One who is best. But why does this matter?

This matters because despite the fact that we were made for something incredible, when we look to substances, people, popularity, fortune, or fame to satisfy our longings, we rob ourselves.

Our generation was made for more, but we are drowning in a sea of pain.

For you, the pain you've known from trying to be in charge might feel insignificant right now. Or you might be experiencing that pain, heavy and horrific, resulting in outright darkness in daily life. No matter where you are coming from, God is calling you to come close and receive a new beginning.

No more suffering in silence.

No more bearing pain alone.

No more feeling helpless or hopeless.

No more hate or self-harm.

Regardless of where you have been, regardless of what you have done, regardless of how convinced you are that you can never, ever change, regardless of how cynical you are to God, he invites you into a relationship with him. A reset for your soul. “Forget about what’s happened,” he says in Isaiah 43:18–19; “don’t keep going over old history. Be alert, be present. I’m about to do something brand-new. It’s bursting out! Don’t you see it? There it is! I’m making a road through the desert, rivers in the badlands.”

No matter how bad your badlands have been, a reset stands ready for you.

Several years ago, I started sharing this reset message on college campuses, in city arenas, local churches, and massive festivals, and truly, the more I’ve seen Jesus work in others’ lives, the more I’ve seen my own need for him to reset me. I’ve seen people from every conceivable background, age group, race, and religion cry out, “Jesus, reset my life!”

Reset my thoughts!

My affections!

My priorities!

My dreams!

My relationships!

My faith!

And each time, I nod my head in agreement, because I need it too.

The beauty of a reset is that it implies a fresh start that was designed by a creator—in this case, Creator God. And based on the texts that come pouring in, every time this message is presented, people are desperate for a fresh start. They are sick and tired of being sick and tired, and they are dying—figuratively and often literally—for a reset, for a shift in perspective, for a brand-new way to live. “If you start with Jesus, everything can change,” I tell them with full confidence. That’s true for them, and also, it’s true for you.

The chapters you're about to read are based on the eight categories that appeared most frequently as we compiled and assessed thousands upon thousands of those text submissions—including the plea for Jesus to reset our faith, plans, self-image, relationships, purity, habits, affections, and generation. Given the breadth of each of these subjects, you'd be correct in assuming the scores of offshoot topics that might fall under each banner. For instance, embedded in the chapter on habits are subtopics such as addictions, compulsions, spiritual disciplines, and lifestyle trends. Within the chapter on resetting my generation, you'll discover how people down through the ages have reset a community, a city, a nation, and an entire culture. Oh, and included in the purity chapter is a lot of talk about sex, if you care to head there first.

Following each chapter is a series of action items I hope you'll take advantage of. They are simple, straightforward, quick-hitting, and based on truth found in God's Word. Write them down and put them into practice. You will not regret it.

Now, to the reset you've been waiting for. If you are truly willing to bring your life, habit, or situation to Jesus, then everything is about to change.

4

Jesus, Reset My Faith

When I was a freshman in college, I was invited by some friends to go on a mission trip to India. I was stoked. The trip was being led by the Luis Palau Association, a global evangelistic ministry based in Portland, Oregon. Luis had come to my hometown a few years prior and had the reputation of being someone who only wanted to talk about Jesus—my kind of guy! A former youth pastor of mine named Dave was leading music for one of the teams and was convinced I needed to be there so that I could learn how to share the gospel from the best. "You are an evangelist," he used to tell me. "What else are you going to live for, Nick? What else matters?"

The invitation came weeks after I had surrendered to God's call for me to preach the gospel, and I remember being shocked that God was dropping me into a ministry environment so fast. When Dave called to explain the purpose and scope of the trip, which included participating in a series of events in southern India that would reach half a million people, I couldn't say no. I was like a giddy middle-school girl as I hung up the phone. Sharing Jesus with half a million people! People living halfway around the world!

My only prior international exposure was my dad driving me three hours north into Canada as a kid, back when you didn't need official documentation to cross the northern border. I hadn't been out of the country since then, I didn't have a passport, and despite my enthusiasm, I highly doubted my parents or college advisor would approve of such an expedition. I prayed simply, "God, if you want me in India, I know you can open the door."

Rain and More Rain

After numerous discussions and prayer sessions with my charmingly overprotective mom, I boarded a plane bound for a place called Total Culture Shock. Two layovers and twenty-seven hours later I arrived in Madurai, India—"temple city," so named for the scores of Hindu and Islamic temples dotting the skyline. At night, I could hear the prayers of Hindus and Muslims rising up from the hills, beckoning their gods, begging for favor, faithfully following the rites of their respective religions. It wasn't only the religious differences I observed that told me I was far from home; there was also my conspicuously white skin. I'm not just white, mind you; I'm North Dakota white. In India, I looked like a lone mini-marshmallow skimming the surface of a sea of hot chocolate, desperately hoping not to get eaten alive.

Our team got settled and organized that first day, meeting with the other teams from around the globe and preparing to forge ahead with our planned events. During the days, we'd split up and go minister in schools or prisons, and during the nights, we'd hold gatherings for the masses. The first night of meetings, we headed down to the outdoor venue that had been set up for the ten thousand people we were expecting, but five minutes into the deal, it was clear only a fraction were going to make it. It was pouring rain—not the best scenario when your venue is a field of mud.

As we looked out over the audience that night, we saw not ten thousand people but rather two hundred people—all of whom were soaked to the bone. It was moving to see the hunger of people walking, many without shoes and none with umbrellas, through the mud and rain to hear the gospel, but it was frustrating that the dismal conditions had kept so many more away. I couldn't have been the only one who felt defeated, deflated, and weak. I wondered why God brought us all this way to set us up to fail. Our team's collective prayers centered on the theme "What is going on, God?"

Scripture tells us that the prophet Elijah had stopped and started rainstorms by prayer, and so we figured if we prayed harder, maybe we could have the same effect. With all our strength, we prayed, we pleaded, and we fell before God. But nope, no dice. It rained the next night too.

God Sees What We Can't See

After three consecutive nights of waterworks, light attendance, and soaked dress shoes, our team was ready to throw in the towel. We wondered what we were doing in India anyway. It all felt so pointless: all this preparation, fundraising, training, and travel—for this? I wanted to go home. With the thick cloud cover day after day, I wasn't even going to have a tan to show for this trip.

Throughout our stay in India, local church leaders served as our hosts and translators. The goal of the mission was to build existing churches and plant new ones with the new believers. On the fourth morning of our event run, an evangelist from Australia who was working in conjunction with our team came into the hotel conference room where we had gathered to pray. Given our dejected state, the Aussie's broad smile and chipper energy as he walked in seemed a little annoying. "Guys!" he said. "You won't believe what I'm about to tell you!"

The only thing any of us wanted to hear was a favorable weather report, although I for one would also have welcomed news of where to find a good hamburger. "Last night I was headed to our outdoor venue with one of our local pastors," he said, "and it was pouring rain again. I asked the pastor if the people in this area thought that their gods were somehow defeating our God . . . and that the awful rainstorms somehow indicated to them that our God was not able to afford everyone a comfortable and dry place to meet."

Our Aussie friend went on. "So, I'm asking the pastor all of these things, and he turns to me and says, 'Haven't you heard? This part of India is dependent on its agriculture, and it hasn't rained in months. People have been dying due to the lack of food in the midst of this drought and famine. As pastors, we believed the hope of Jesus proclaimed would lift the people's hearts, so we promoted this campaign throughout this entire region. The promotion was so successful that whether people had any interest in coming, everyone knew that these events would commence on January 28. And on the day of January 28, the very evening the promoted events were to begin, the heavens opened, and the rain poured down.'" Our Aussie colleague then said, "At this, the pastor turned to me, ecstatic, saying, 'People don't think their gods are defeating yours. Not at all! Word is spreading through the villages that the God of the Christians has brought the rain.'"

We thought God needed our voices when all he needed was our presence. We had placed our hope in the power of small sound systems to carry a message, when God intended to use the sound system of the heavens all along. As the evangelist's update soaked into our team's minds and hearts, we couldn't help but laugh. How had we totally spaced the fact that God always has purposes beyond what we can see? We felt like total jerks before God. If we'd prayed then and there on the spot, we would have said, "Here we are, your beloved idiots. We'll never question you again."

Eventually, the rains did stop during that trip, and in the end, more than fifty thousand people (that we know of) surrendered their lives to Jesus. More than that, all of southern India had been exposed to our miracle-working God. On the flight home, I remember thinking, *You just never know with God.* You never fully know what he is up to, who he is after, how he is working all things together for good. I love to think about what it will be like in heaven, where we'll have greater perspective on all that happened down here. I picture getting to watch a highlight reel of my life and seeing things from God's all-encompassing point of view. Every six seconds, I'll be saying, "Oh, wow. That's what that was about. I was complaining the whole time that experience unfolded, but now I can see . . . that was amazing!"

While we're still living these earthbound lives, however, we don't tend to consider the hard things that happen to us as very amazing at all, which is why faith is so critical to a person trying to follow Jesus. Faith is seeing things through God's perspective rather than our own.

The Crux of Faith

Hebrews 11 is called the faith chapter and it defines faith as "confidence in what we hope for and assurance about what we do not see" (verse 1, NIV). While confidence and assurance sound great, for many people these terms have nothing to do with their actual faith. When it comes to the practical, day-to-day existence you and I and everyone else is trying to hold together, faith doesn't often factor in. Confidence in what we hope for? Nah, we'd rather place confidence in where we've been, what we've already done, what is real, what is known. Assurance about what we do not see? No, thanks. We're only sure about what our five senses detect.

In verse 2, we learn that faith is what "distinguished our ancestors" and "set them above the crowd." And Hebrews 11:6 says that without faith it is impossible to please God. So, apparently we need faith. And yet when we truly look up and down the line of ancestors the writer of Hebrews is talking about, do we really want to be like them? I already told you what a lunatic people thought Noah was. People probably regarded Abraham the very same way. Do you ever wonder what this kind of radical faith would look like today?

Imagine some seventy-five-year-old man—we'll call him Warren—who suddenly started having visions. He couldn't explain what was happening. Was his wife trying some new ingredients in her beef casserole? Had he been getting enough sleep? Soon after the visions came, a voice said to him, "Leave everything. Pack what you can. Grab your family, and hit the road. I will give you directions later."

Can you imagine if Warren was your uncle or grandfather and called to give you the news that he was going to ditch all his earthly possessions—his home, his car, his sweet La-Z-Boy recliner—and head off to who-knows-where and possibly live there for the rest of his life? I think most of us would think it was time to put Uncle Warren in a nursing home. And yet my story of Warren is basically just that of Abraham in Genesis 12, the guy known as the father of our faith. At age seventy-five, he was called by God to leave everything. Perhaps more astounding still, he said yes.

If we are invited into an adventure with Jesus, then why is our first instinct to turn to human reason rather than to divine intervention? We typically don't see life situations through the lens of faith. If we did, we would see from a totally different perspective.

I've planned PULSE events over the years that make zero sense in terms of timelines and budgets. Zero sense. And yet I knew that God was calling us to do it, and I knew that he would find a way to make it work. In the end, he always did, even as more than a handful of people watching me were muttering "Nut job" under their breath. And you know what? I don't fault them. Think about it: we who have surrendered our lives to Jesus are following a guy who voluntarily was executed on a cross after healing the sick and giving sight to the blind. He raised people from the dead and was himself raised from the dead, and then he went back up to heaven, where he came from, and sat down at the right hand of his Dad. In his wake, he said that everyone who follows him should also be excited about death. We should die to our self-focused wishes and ways, our ideas and our dreams, and we should devote every minute of every day to him.

Huh? Who does this? Some people say that it's radical to go party and live a life of rebellion, but there's nothing radical about that life. Everyone is doing that. Do you want to be really radical? Follow Jesus! Lay down your one and only life. Die to yourself, and live for God.

My Buddy Jazer

While it might seem crazy, I see a movement of people running from worldly wisdom and straight to Jesus. Take my buddy Jazer (pronounced YAH-sir). Between the ages of seventeen and nineteen, Jazer was chasing anything and everything that the world offered—women, money, drinking, partying, sex. He had denied the faith he held to as a kid and run as far away from Jesus as he could. His family had immigrated to the United States from El Salvador, and while family members were glad to be in this country, it took them some time to get on their feet. During that in-between season, Jazer, his parents, and his sister lived in a tiny shed in some family's backyard—essentially homeless and certainly poor.

Eventually, Jazer figured out that the American Dream was less a dream and more a nightmare. A series of experiences and relationships left him feeling broken and isolated. He knew he needed to change, but he didn't know where to start. Enter a group of people who love Jesus and who love Jazer and who were willing to speak truth into his life. They invited him to a few gatherings of other believers and stood by his side as he made his way back to God. He'd always been a charismatic guy who was charming and smart, and over time he sensed God was asking him to use those gifts to glorify God instead of using them to land his next date.

Today, right this minute as I write this chapter, Jazer is on a bus, traveling all over the country to challenge and rally students in forty cities who want to gather with us on the National Mall for Together 2016. He's encouraging them to rally together for a worthwhile cause. He's challenging them to pray. And he's teaching them how to renew their faith when that faith has grown ineffective and smug.

Jazer's own faith was renewed a few years ago, and now he's showing others how to stop running and return home.

Thriving in a Faith-Fueled Life

Most people I talk to have had a Jazer season at one point in their lives or another, when they wake up and feel disillusioned with God and aren't all that interested in having Jesus for a friend. Maybe they used to love God, but now they're indifferent. Maybe they used to be passionate about seeing lives transformed in the name of Jesus, but now they're lacking that hunger and are coasting through life. Maybe they used to feel excited about the adventure of going God's way, but now they're skeptical about whether he really cares for them at all. Or maybe they never had real faith to begin with and are sick and tired of being let down.

No matter where we are coming from, a fresh perspective is available. We can do more than check the box on the form marked Christian. We can experience and know Jesus. We can actually thrive in a faith-fueled life.

The same invitation is offered to you, right now, as you read these words.

If you are tired of living for nothing more than your hopes, your dreams, your desires, and your needs, and you want to start living beyond yourself, Jesus stands ready to reset your faith. If you are bored from praying prayers that you can manage on your own and want to start boldly petitioning all of heaven to radically change your world, Jesus stands ready to reset your faith. If you've had it with singing "How great is our God" and then living like he's really, really small, Jesus stands ready to reset your faith. If you've grown cynical about whether God still lives and moves and breathes in and through his people, whether there are still miracles in our midst, whether your life is destined for more than a lackluster existence that tragically resembles a gerbil running his scrawny legs ragged on a wheel going nowhere fast, Jesus stands ready to reset your faith. And if I were a betting man, I'd wager that once you allowed him to reset your faith, you'd stand by the choice you made.

When my friends and I started PULSE, it felt like we were praying nonstop. We used to say, "We are either prayerful or prideful," as we gathered and tried to keep first things first. We all had been a part of enough lifeless prayer meetings along the way to know that we wanted ours to feel different. We wanted ours to yield results beyond simply being updated on the latest Christian gossip. And so, taking a page from the early church, we flipped to Acts 1 and began reading one chapter at a time about how the followers of Jesus were formed and how they learned to walk by faith. We would read a chapter and use it as prayer fuel for the week. When we landed at Acts 2:41, where it says that on one day, more than three thousand people were added to the church, we stopped and prayed, "God, we want to see three thousand people added to your church in one day! We want to believe you like those early followers believed you. We want to have that kind of crazy faith."

As students who had been good Western Christians for many years, we all knew how easy it was to play it safe, to resist anything that would demand us to stretch, change, or risk. Our collective response was to beg God to keep us far from fine—you know, a life that's fine, a job that's fine, a day that's fine. We wanted much more than fine. We wanted to have the sort of impact that could only be explained in terms of faith, in terms of God's activity in and through our lives.

Not surprisingly, the more we prayed for our faith to be increased so that we could *see* the reality of Jesus and *savor* the reality of Jesus and *share* the reality of Jesus with other people, the more we experienced a sense of sureness that God was guiding us and protecting us and inviting us to go deeper with him. Faith redefines safety to be the moments of God-dependence rather than the moments that don't require God at all.

It was terrifying from time to time, but walking by faith and not by sight should be terrifying. And yet, in the same way that being blindfolded for that silly game you played as a kid allows you to feel a rush of excitement over having to find your way sight unseen, there is much more to life when we're stumbling hard after God. Life is lived only when we live a life that is bigger than ourselves. That's what faith is all about. As a friend of mine once said, faith is spelled R-I-S-K. There is no growth inside the comfort zone, and outside the comfort zone is where faith thrives.

Bold Like Habakkuk

After that trip to India, I studied the book of Habakkuk for the first time. (To find it, head to the end of the Old Testament and go left five books.) The story reeled me in right away because chapter 1 opens with Habakkuk, a prophet, complaining to God about all of the injustice, hardship, and depravity he saw in the world around him. "Why do you make me look at injustice?" he ranted in Habakkuk 1:3 (NIV). "Why do you tolerate wrongdoing? Destruction and violence are before me; there is strife, and conflict abounds."

I read Habakkuk's words and immediately found a friend. As I surveyed the landscape of my college campus, I saw nothing but darkness, racial tension, drunkenness, and strife. Habakkuk would fire off his complaint to God, and I'd sit there with my open Bible in my lap going, "Yeah. What he said, God. Doeth what he sayeth!"

In Habakkuk 1:5 (NIV), God replies to the prophet, saying, "Watch—and be utterly amazed. For I am going to do something in your days that you would not believe, even if you were told."

Still, Habakkuk wasn't so sure. And so he geared up for yet another complaint of God. Chapter 1, verse 13 (NIV): "Your eyes are too pure to look on evil" writes the prophet. "You cannot tolerate wrongdoing. Why then do you tolerate the treacherous? Why are you silent while the wicked swallow up those more righteous than themselves?" I love this guy's courage, don't you? He is so confident in his understanding of the way things should be that he's holding God accountable. Talk about a bold move.

Well, God offers a rebuttal to that complaint too, and this time, his reassurance works. It's good to note here that when arguing with God, there is really only one outcome. Which brings me to my favorite part of the story. In Habakkuk 3:2 (NIV), we read the prophet's prayer as his heart and perspective have been shifted, literally reset. These are his final words back to God. "LORD, I have heard of your fame," he says. "I stand in awe of your deeds, LORD. Repeat them in our day, in our time make them known."

As college students, Habakkuk 3:2 became more than just a verse to us. It became our anthem. Habakkuk said, "LORD, I have heard of your fame . . ." You see, some people are content to hear about God—all the stories of Moses and the Red Sea, of Joshua and the battle of Jericho, of David and Goliath, of the Virgin Mary and Baby Jesus—but never let those life stories impact their own. Habakkuk took it to the next level when he said, "I stand in awe of your deeds." Certainly, it's a common occurrence to hear stories of God's power and goodness and to be swept into an awestruck posture of worship as a result. But Habakkuk 3:2 models a third dimension.

1. Habakkuk hears of God's fame.
2. Habakkuk stands in awe of God's deeds.
3. Habakkuk asks God to do it in his day.

For Habakkuk, faith-fueled living demanded more than following the status quo. The stories of God's faithfulness compelled Habakkuk to worship God for who he is and for all that he had done. And that awestruck experience compelled Habakkuk to call on that same wonder-working God to show himself in his day. In response to this model we would cry out to heaven, "God, we want to see it. We need a movement of your Spirit today. Do it again, through us!"

In the same way that I couldn't see the purpose behind the three-day water party during my trip to India, Habakkuk couldn't see God's purpose in allowing sin to go unchecked on the earth. Yet in both cases we see a common thread in the character of God. While we always focus on God changing our circumstance, God is always focused on changing us.

I'm reminded here of Psalm 24, which confirms that the earth is the Lord's and everything in it—including "the world and all its people" (verse 1, NLT), which, by definition includes you and me. Faith says, "God, I trust you to be God in my life. I will walk with you even when I can't see where we're going. I will trust you with all of my days."

One Hundred Revelations

I'm sure that another reason I appreciated Habakkuk's story is that throughout my teenage years, I experienced dozens of times when I paused momentarily and took stock of my life and of the world spinning around me and thought, *Something's not right here. Something needs to change.* I went to Bible camp most summers when I was a kid and was always brought to my knees, literally and figuratively, by the talks those pastors would give. I'd go to youth conferences from time to time, where I would be invited to take stock of my relationship with God. Was I really living for him? Did I care about what really mattered in life? One time while I was in middle school, my parents bought me a ticket to go to an event called Heaven's Gates and Hell's Flames, and I remember going forward at the end of the presentation, tears streaming down my face, ready to rededicate myself to God. At the time, the worst sin I was committing was probably something like rolling my eyes at my mom, but at the time my waywardness felt very dramatic, like most things do when you're growing up.

Those revelations I made during middle school and high school helped me make sense of a trend that I notice still today, which is that I never stop needing to choose faith. I'm always going to follow Jesus imperfectly, which means I'm always going to need to take stock: Am I really living for God right now? Am I open to his will and ways? Does my heart truly beat for the things he values? Am I walking by faith or by sight?

Whenever I close a PULSE event and invite people to respond to the gospel of Jesus, I'm simultaneously responding to him too. I never ask someone else to do what I'm not doing myself—over and over again. To be clear, I am not questioning my salvation, but rather who has my heart. Every day, I must surrender to having faith, to trusting and believing Jesus. These things aren't relevant in my life only once, but rather all day, every day, for all the days I'm alive. Today, right now, I need Jesus. Faith is the air we inhale into our lungs, knowing that the moment we choose to neglect the act, that last breath really will be our last. We say yes to faith, Hebrews 11:6 reminds us, because without it we'll never please God.

Faith in Everyday Life

You don't hang out in my line of work without coming across some pretty cool stories of God rewarding faithful followers of his. People often tell me they think a life of faith is boring, and I always tell them they couldn't be more wrong. People may be boring. Churches may be boring. If you come to a

PULSE event, from time to time I may even be boring. But Jesus? He's never boring. Life with Jesus is always on fire.

For example, a couple in Winona, Minnesota, who decided not to remodel their kitchen but instead use those funds to support some kids who wanted to come to an event to hear about Jesus . . . do you think that couple was bored after hearing that a few of those kids they sponsored surrendered their lives to him?

Or a group of students from Oshkosh, Wisconsin, who drained their bank accounts—meager though those totals were—to host a night of worship for their unbelieving friends . . . do you think they were bored upon seeing their classmates make radical decisions that night to follow Jesus?

Or the family of a young woman named Amy, who fell ill at age twenty-seven with double pneumonia and was declared the "sickest person in the entire Twin Cities." Family members sidestepped all the doom-and-gloom prognoses in favor of calling as many people all across the world together in prayer for this woman as they possibly could . . . do you think they were bored the day their daughter/sister/niece emerged from her forty-day coma and was miraculously restored to full health?

Or a successful business friend of mine in Bismarck, North Dakota, who decided to live on 10 percent of his income and give the rest away to see revival explode in this nation . . . do you think his family is bored when receiving reports of how his dollars are resulting in lives changed, communities transformed, and the hope of Jesus being advanced?

Or the guy who said yes to God's call on his life to reach his entire generation with the good news of the gospel, even though he had no experience, no platform, no money, and no clearly defined strengths . . . do you think he was bored the moment he realized that within the first five years of ministry, he'd already spoken to more people than lived in his entire state? (I can answer that one for you. He wasn't bored; I know, because the guy is me.)

So many magnificent stories exist of those following faithfully after God—

laying it all on the line, placing full confidence in that which we can only hope for, choosing to be sure in that which is unseen. And time and time again, God shows up, parting waters, providing resources, coming through. Sometimes it's at the eleventh hour, I'll grant you, which will always be a mystery to me. Like, why can't God come through at the third hour? Or the sixth hour? Or even the ninth hour? Why does he have to wait until we're freaking out inside? This is when I cue that heavenly image: "Oh, wow. So that's what that was about."

Personally, I think God is just so clear on the fact that faith is critical to a meaningful life. Growth doesn't happen in the comfort zone; it happens only when our faith is being stretched.

Ready for a Reset?

If you're in need of a fresh perspective, maybe an infusion of faith in God, I'd like to offer you a starting point. His name is Jesus.

While it might sound simplistic, your faith is entirely dependent on Jesus. It's not about you fixing yourself. It's not about you figuring it all out. It's not about you being good enough. Faith is simply about turning to Jesus. After the faith chapter of Hebrews 11 comes the good news in Hebrews 12:2 that reminds us that Jesus is the author and perfecter of our faith. The Author writes it, and the Perfecter completes it.

From start to finish, it's about Jesus. He lived the life you could not live and died the death you deserve. If you've never trusted Jesus as your Savior, if you've never surrendered your life to his care and asked him to cleanse you from your sin, then I want you to know that you can make that decision right now. You can turn to him right now, "Jesus, I am turning to you. Forgive me for the life I've lived apart from you. I am sorry. I confess I have done wrong against you. I believe you died on the cross for me and that you defeated my sin and death when you rose from the grave. Right now I surrender to you. Reset my life.

Take over. Be the leader of my life. Fill me with you Holy Spirit. Help me to follow you."

If you turn to Jesus, the Bible says you are made new. You are no longer under any obligation to live the same life, but instead you are being set free. And it's free people who can walk by faith.

I'm going to close this chapter following the example set by Habakkuk 3:2.

Review the Evidence

Take some time to go back through the stories that highlight God's power and glory in your life. Grab a journal or your smartphone and start a list of evidences of God's faithfulness in your life. Think back across the years and experiences of your life. How has God been faithful to you? When has he shown up in your life? If nothing else, you've got two entries waiting: (1) You're alive, and (2) You're loved. Start there and work backward. Be reminded of his consistent care for you.

Renew the Awe

Next, ask God to renew your amazement over who he is and all he has done. I will often encourage people to do whatever is necessary for them to enter a state of worship:

Turn on some Hillsong music, listen to a Francis Chan sermon, sit quietly for a few minutes. Once the static of life subsides and you are still before God, open your Bible to Psalm 24 (below), and ask him what he wants you to learn.

> The earth is the LORD's, and everything in it,
>   the world, and all who live in it;
> for he founded it on the seas
>   and established it on the waters.

Who may ascend the mountain of the Lord?
  Who may stand in his holy place?
The one who has clean hands and a pure heart,
  who does not trust in an idol
  or swear by a false god.

They will receive blessing from the Lord
  and vindication from God their Savior.
Such is the generation of those who seek him,
  who seek your face, God of Jacob.

Lift up your heads, you gates;
  be lifted up, you ancient doors,
  that the King of glory may come in.
Who is this King of glory?
  The Lord strong and mighty,
  the Lord mighty in battle.
Lift up your heads, you gates;
  lift them up, you ancient doors,
  that the King of glory may come in.
Who is he, this King of glory?
  The Lord Almighty—
  he is the King of glory.
  (Psalm 24, NIV)

I would challenge you to read from the Psalms daily for a proper attitude of worship. Stop as something stands out to you. What about God's character does the text reveal to you, and why? What qualities make him worthy of your trust?

Reaffirm Your Trust

Finally, like Habakkuk did, dream big and ask God to perform miracles, part the seas, and show his power right here, right now, in your life. And then go wherever God says to go. It's one thing to pray big prayers. It's something completely different to put feet to those prayers. God is looking for people listening for his voice and ready to respond. I tell people this and immediately get pushback: "But how will I know if it's really the voice of God?" they want to know. "How can I be sure I'm getting it right?"

To which I say, "Listen. If you're prompted to give money away, or get up early to lead a Bible study, or plan an event for your friends to hear about Jesus, or take your entire spring break to go on a missions trip to Africa, or any of a thousand other noble, wonderful things . . . quit fretting over whether it's God you're hearing. For all those waiting for the audible voice of God to show up in your life, consider this your moment. God is calling you to go."

Okay, to be fair, it may just be me telling you to go. And on occasion, you will respond to an emotion and it won't be God. But in my experience, these occasions are rare. I want to encourage you that whenever you are compelled to set aside your wants, desires, money, or reputation and consider other people's needs ahead of your own, there is a pretty good chance it is God somehow moving in your life. Because really, when would your selfish self choose to do anything that wasn't solely about you? My point here is to trust Jesus to activate your faith, and then be ready to respond as soon as he does. Oh, and as you pray for opportunities, don't be surprised when the opportunities begin to show up.

I came across a great quote from the Christian and Missionary Alliance founder A. B. Simpson recently, which read, "On to broader fields of holy vision, / On to loftier heights of faith and love; / Onward, upward, wholly apprehending / All for which He calls thee from above."[33]

It's my prayer that as you seek out this reset, your journey toward deeper faith would lift your eyes to the only place where true help is found.

5

Jesus, Reset My Plans

I met Marilyn in the lobby of the church in Fargo, North Dakota, where I grew up. The day we met, I had recently returned from that trip to India I mentioned earlier and was asked by my pastor to give a report to the congregation on how things went. He had given me three minutes to share, but I'm pretty sure I filled fifteen. How could I not? I was that excited over having witnessed more than three hundred thousand people hear about Jesus.

"Nick, you don't know me," Marilyn began, when she approached me after the church service, "but I know your family. I'm from Langdon, North Dakota, and I grew up with your parents."

Just south of the Canadian border lies a town in Cavalier County called Langdon. With a population of only two thousand people, it's the kind of place you need to be planning to see to actually see. Langdon isn't really on the way to anything, and if you don't need a Hot Stuff pizza from the SuperPumper gas station at the only stoplight in town, you might miss it altogether.

"Nick, as you were up there speaking," Marilyn continued, "I kept hearing a voice in my head saying, 'Nick needs to come to Langdon . . . Nick needs to come to Langdon.'"

Wait. What did she just say?

While I've never been the most detailed person, I am one of the most driven and focused you will probably meet. I have a musician friend who once called me the "Dakota Bulldog" because I was the kind of guy who got an idea in his teeth and wouldn't let it go. With that said, as God was whispering to me during a prayer session in India, I had actually mapped out a plan to go speak in Langdon. This was uncanny! The one hitch was that it was my plan, due to unfold in my way. God would have something to say about that in coming days.

Back in India, I was on my knees, asking God to move across the region, when I was taken in my mind's eye back to that tiny town of Langdon. As I got my bearings in the vision, I was at some kind of event in town with a band playing and there were a few hundred people there. I was sure it was a few hundred people because for Langdon this was the equivalent of a standing-room-only stadium for the latest Taylor Swift concert. Huge. In my vision, all of my relatives were there, my cousins, my aunts, my uncles, my grandparents on both sides. They were all at this event together, along with the rest of town. And I was there sharing the gospel for all of Langdon to hear.

Now, I'm not sure how you would respond to a vision like that. For me, it was a mixture of elation and terror. The thought of standing in front of those I loved most and talking about such an important message was enough to make me nauseous. I had yet to start PULSE. I wasn't speaking anywhere yet. I was barely old enough to drive. How was I supposed to accomplish such a gigantic goal?

I pulled open my journal and to the best of my ability began to lay out a game plan. "I will go back to school and finish college," I scribbled. "After college, I will complete seminary training. After I'm trained through seminary, I will go to Langdon. I'm in."

When Our Plans Get "Altared"

In the book of Proverbs, the wisest man who ever lived, Solomon, looked at the state of affairs surrounding him and penned words that summed up what he saw: "In their hearts humans plan their course, but the Lord establishes their steps" (Proverbs 16:9, niv). I was stranded one time somewhere in Montana, and with more than a little frustration motivating me, I abridged those verses in my mind: "We make our plans, and God cancels our flights!" I was pretty sure God was asleep at the wheel while I needed to get somewhere fast. In the moment, my plans always seem best to me. My way or the highway, right? Solomon had learned that wasn't a very good posture to have.

Of all the difficult things God asks us to surrender, our plans tend to top the list. Especially for planners, being spontaneous and flexible and adaptable seems about as fun as homework on a Saturday. For a planner, every obligation ushers in a whole series of concerns: "I need to know where we are going, when we are going there, how long we are staying, when we are coming back, what we will do while we're there, what I need to wear, how I need to prepare . . ." and on and on it goes. They like certainty. Predictability. The safety of having a plan. And yet with God, one of the first things he asks us to place on the figurative altar of surrender is exactly that: our plan.

As far as planners go, a guy named Saul was about as focused, and also as gifted, as they come. He worked hard, studied hard, worked harder, studied harder, slept a few hours, and then was back at it again. Saul had been raised in the "right" family and been given amazing opportunities for success from a young age. He landed in the best school, and then the best internship, and then the best job, where he quickly rose through the ranks. I'm taking some creative license here in portraying the Saul of the Scriptures, but you get the point. This guy was headed for greatness, and nothing was going to hold him back. "You know my pedigree," he once wrote of himself. "A legitimate birth, circumcised on the eighth day; an Israelite from the elite tribe of Benjamin; a strict and devout adherent to God's law; a fiery defender of the purity of my religion, even to the point of persecuting the church; a meticulous observer of everything set down in God's law Book" (Philippians 3:5). In other words, he was from the right tribe, he kept his nose clean, he worked harder than everyone else, and he was the best. Except that he wasn't living for Jesus.

Saul was on mission like a dog sniffing out a bone, when he was abruptly stopped in his tracks. He was making his way to a town called Damascus, to bring justice to those who were disobeying the law. Unfortunately, in this case, those people happened to be Christians. He didn't *want* to kill Christians; he *had* to kill Christians. They. Were. Breaking. God's. Law.

So, en route to this mission, as Saul plowed ahead with fire in his gut, the last thing he expected to have happen was for his plan to get interrupted by Jesus. And yet that's exactly what went down.

"Saul," a simple voice whispered his way. "Saul, why do you persecute me?" (This story is found in Acts 9.)

Saul (whose name was soon to be changed to Paul) would quickly learn that God's plan for his life included not killing believers but rather loving them and leading them well. Talk about a reset plan! This was one for the ages, revealed before he even knew to ask for it. And yet the apostle Paul would go on to impact the world for Jesus in utterly unparalleled ways. He established foundational truths of the Christian faith (like the idea that even if we're really, really good people, we are still saved by faith in Jesus alone); he led three wide-reaching missionary journeys, catalyzing the conversions of thousands of people; he penned much of the New Testament . . . I'd say this guy was the real deal. His story ended the way every story ends, when that story is surrendered to Jesus. It goes down in history as a story of power and impact, of goodness and godliness and grace.

What's (Actually) Up

In the Old Testament book of Job, the prophet of the same name cries out to God after all of his plans have been dashed. If you think your plans have been shaken up from time to time, go spend some time with my buddy Job. He lost his house, his job, his car, his health, and even his children. He basically lost everything except for his wife, who wasn't exactly a positive force in his life. In response to seeing all that God had allowed her husband to lose, she told Job to "Curse God and die!" (Job 2:9, NIV).

As Job sat in the rubble formerly known as his life, trying to tell God what's up, three of his "friends" stop by to tell Job what's up. They take it upon themselves to shoot straight with their buddy about how the world works and about how he got himself into such a sorry state. They may have had good intentions, but their words are poisonous to Job—not to mention highly offensive to God. A few minutes into the friends' boneheaded remarks, God has had enough. "Why do you talk without knowing what you're talking about?" he thunders from the heavens.

He continues,

Pull yourself together, Job!
    Up on your feet! Stand tall!
I have some questions for you,
    and I want some straight answers.
Where were you when I created the earth?
    Tell me, since you know so much!
Who decided on its size? Certainly you'll know that!
    Who came up with the blueprints and measurements?
How was its foundation poured,
    and who set the cornerstone,

While the morning stars sang in chorus
    and all the angels shouted praise?
And who took charge of the ocean
    when it gushed forth like a baby from the womb?
That was me! I wrapped it in soft clouds,
    and tucked it in safely at night.
Then I made a playpen for it,
    a strong playpen so it couldn't run loose,
And said, "Stay here, this is your place.
    Your wild tantrums are confined to this place."
    (Job 38:1–11)

Essentially, God tells everyone to shut up, reads a few lines from his résumé, drops the mike, and walks off stage to a standing ovation while everyone in the crowd says, "Now that . . . that's what's up."

Like Job and his friends, you and I tend to think we know what's best. And so we plan. And work. And plan. And live. And plan. And achieve. And plan some more from there. Before long, we are hip deep in the American Dream with only a boatload of debt to show for it, thinking, "Hold up. This wasn't the plan."

To which God says, "I have a better plan, if you're interested. You can trust me. I've done some pretty cool stuff before, and I'm committed to doing cool stuff again."

Going All-In with God

Early in PULSE's existence, my friends and I were faced with the decision of prioritizing safety and preservation or the voice of God. (Clearly, God's voice can sometimes direct us toward safety and preservation, but the sum of Scripture reveals those times as exceptions instead of the rule.) The reason it was such a hot topic for us in those first days and months was that as a ministry we were nearly broke. We had raised enough personal support to pay our apartment rent for a few months, but we weren't nearly where we needed to be to pull off our second big event. So fresh off our starting mark, we had to decide, "Do we want PULSE to last, or do we want to do this event?"

To some, the answer would have been easy: "Events come and go, but organizations are what last." In fact, this was exactly the advice we were getting from all sides. Very Smart People were saying we should make decisions to keep ourselves afloat, which is exactly the logic played out in churches and homes all around this big, beautiful globe. "We can't take on this project because the funds aren't there," the thinking goes. "We can't go on that mission trip because it doesn't fit with where we are headed as a family." Ironically, the very decisions that once seemed God-honoring can become the biggest obstacles to our hearing from God.

For my own part, after much prayer and contemplation, I went to my team with the simple question, "What if PULSE ends? How did we get here, and why are we doing this anyway?" As we talked through the scenarios, we remembered that we had never started PULSE to launch an organization or to get paid. If we were after safety, then there were far better career options to chase. No, we launched PULSE because God called us to impact our generation for him. And now, only a few months into our existence, we were going to pull back from our mission? All because we wanted to play it safe?

We made a decision then and there that if PULSE was going to end, we were completely fine with that. God didn't need PULSE; he could easily raise up other vehicles to accomplish his goals. And even if PULSE ended, our commitment to the task wouldn't change. We would start something else or join another cause. We existed for a singular mission, and we were going to give everything we had until it was accomplished.

"If we are going down, we are going down swinging," our slogan became, and many times it felt like we were headed precisely there. And yet God never allowed us to fall. (So far, anyway!)

Recently I gathered our staff as we laid out plans for what will be our craziest year yet and opened the meeting with a reminder. "We love you," I said. "That is the truth. But what's also true is that PULSE does not exist to pay team members. We exist to reach this generation. And if we need to choose between making payroll or doing an event we feel God has called us to do, we will do the event every time." Team members started nodding their heads. Why? Because they get it. Our first loyalty is to sharing Jesus. We leave our payroll in his hands. In some small sense, it's our way of declaring that we prize our Planner more than our plans.

Jesus once said to his disciples, "Anyone who intends to come with me has to let me lead. You're not in the driver's seat; *I* am. Don't run from suffering; embrace it. Follow me and I'll show you how. Self-help is no help at all. Self-sacrifice is the way, my way, to finding yourself, your true self. What kind of deal is it to get everything you want but lose yourself? What could you ever trade your soul for?" (Matthew 16:24–26). We find life when we lose it, we find help when we're helpless, and we find the best plan we've ever known the day we surrender our plans to him. "He is no fool who gives what he cannot keep to gain that which he cannot lose,"[34] missionary Jim Elliot once journaled. Mr. Elliot would be killed in 1956 while on mission to reach a tribe in South America that didn't know God, but news of his death would launch a missions movement that continues to impact the world today. I'm willing to bet he's not wishing he'd taken the safe route, there from his new home in heaven at Jesus' side.

"Count your life as nothing for my sake," God says to us. "And I'll make it count in ways you never could."

"My ways are not your ways," God whispers to us. "But trust me: you're going to like my ways more."

The Reset to God's Good Plans

Saying yes to Jesus means more than checking a box. It means following him every day, saying no to self and yes to Jesus. And while sticking to our plan may give the feeling of security, unless the plan has been laid before the Lord, it could be leading down a dead-end path.

Let's be honest for a moment. Is your plan really that great, anyway? Is it really as foolproof as you'd like others to believe? Or, like most of us, does even your best-case scenario keep you up at night as you wonder if things are actually going to pan out in the end? Could it be that God has a better plan? If he offered his consulting services pro bono, would you take them?

God once said to the prophet Jeremiah, "For I know the plans I have for you . . . , plans to prosper you and not to harm you, plans to give you hope and a future" (Jeremiah 29:11, NIV), and while most people have that verse highlighted in a Bible somewhere, I wonder how often we remember who it is that provides true prosperity, true hope, and a true future. It's God! We don't underline that verse because we are encouraged by our own abilities; we underline it because we are encouraged by his. We are amazed to think that there could actually be a future and a hope for us, beyond the awkward phases of puberty and beyond.

I often hear people say that our culture needs to change . . . and change radically. And while I agree with the assessment, I come away thinking, *How can we expect a radical change from God if we are not willing to live radically changed lives?* As the saying goes, "If you keep doing what you've always done, you are going to keep getting what you've always gotten." If your current life pattern has you living life with Jesus to the full, then keep at it. But if your plans have taken precedent over the Planner, then hold up. It might be time to reset. Now, I'm not saying to jump ship; I'm just suggesting you reach for a compass.

Getting to Langdon

As I stood there listening to Marilyn, I could hardly believe what she was saying. Nowhere in my talk had I mentioned visiting Langdon or any visions I'd had of the sort. (My home church wasn't into visions. They would have thought I was crazy, at best.) I hadn't told anyone about that vision, and aside from my journal entry from that day when God spoke to me, no record of it existed anywhere. I was pretty sure Marilyn hadn't broken into my dorm room in Minneapolis, stolen my journal, and driven through the night back to Fargo to hear me speak. But what was the explanation here? How did she know that God was asking me to come to Langdon?

These questions were bouncing around in my brain as Marilyn continued. "Nick," she said, "I'm going to go back to Langdon and organize an event for the summer. We will promote it everywhere. We will get a band and have you come share the gospel. I think we can get the whole town there. Will you come?"

I was speechless. This wasn't how this was supposed to go down. I was supposed to go finish college and then go to seminary and then . . .

Or was I?

As I stood there in the lobby of my church, all I could do was smile. This plan—from God, evidently—was so much cooler than my plan had been. Not to mention much quicker. He had laid a dream on my heart while I was halfway around the world that would then get confirmed back in Fargo, my hometown, within one week's time. No human had brokered the deal. This was God's doing, all alone.

"Of course," I said to Marilyn. "Totally. Let's do this."

I never did tell Marilyn about that vision, but that very summer, I did make it to Langdon. And following the talk I gave before a crowd that included my cousins, my aunts, my uncles, and both sets of grandparents, more than thirty people surrendered their lives to Jesus. Even if I'd had my seminary degree at the time, I can't imagine things could have gone better than that. "Unless the Lord builds the house, the builders labor in vain," Solomon once said (Psalm 127:1, NIV). God's plan is always worth pursuing above our own.

Still today, I keep a note on my desk that I received at that Langdon event, which represented the first time I'd shared the gospel at an outreach in the United States. It reads,

> I have prayed for years for Langdon, that someday all would hear clearly the message of Jesus Christ. My humble approach to sharing my faith to those I had grown up with over the years has been weak, to say the least. Thank you, for being the answer to my prayers, for boldly speaking the Truth and leaving nothing on the table. It was an awesome weekend for the people of Langdon, including my family. The community has been blessed and many saved by your ministry, your music, your love for Christ, and your sacrifice of time. Knowing firsthand how rare an event like this is, the cards were stacked heavily against you guys. This weekend is clearly proof once again that with Christ, absolutely anything is possible. Love you, Nick.

That note will always be invaluable to me, because it was written by my dad.

Ready for a Reset?

So, I wonder: What is it for you? What plans are you clutching so tightly that you think you might just die if they get thwarted or changed? Maybe you're in high school and determined to be part of that team, that group, that club. Or maybe you're a college co-ed who's pursuing your major, your dreams, your plans, your future Mr. or Mrs. Right. Maybe you're a businessperson who's on the fast track, according to plan. There is nothing wrong with being focused; I'm simply asking which is more important to you—the Planner or the plan. We can become so focused on *it* (whatever "it" is), that we forget what it *is all about.* Life is all about Jesus.

If you're interested in a reset in this area of life, then spend some time answering these four questions. Tell God the truth about where you are.

1. Are there goals, dreams, involvements, or plans that I have placed above God in my life?
2. Are there things I'm committed to that might be keeping me from hearing his voice?
3. Am I truly willing to give all in order to follow Jesus' plans for me?
4. Am I open to receiving the type of success he has for me?

Then pray a simple prayer of surrender to God, letting go of your plans and opening your hands to what he has for you—his way, in his time. There are few things more important in life than being confident we are exactly where God wants us to be.

6

Jesus, Reset My Self-Image

Call me old-fashioned, but I still love Facebook. Maybe it's because the story of its founding took place around the same time we were launching PULSE.

I caught the Facebook-related movie *The Social Network* when it came out a few years ago, and while many of the exchanges were memorable, its final scene struck a real chord with me. Did you see it? The actor playing Mark Zuckerberg is sitting in a conference room alone, after his attorney has just walked out. His laptop is on the table in front of him, and Zuckerberg is inviting the coveted Erica Albright to be his Facebook friend. A dialogue box pops up, telling Mark that Erica will have to confirm that they are friends before she will be added to his network, and so he slumps down into his chair, his eyes fixed on this screen, and starts refreshing his screen every few seconds, over and over again.

No matter your preferred social-media outlet—Facebook, Twitter, Instagram, Snapchat, Periscope, or whatever the latest toy is—we've all been swept into the world of likes, comments, and friend requests. As I watched *The Social*

Network and imagined Mark Zuckerberg, the Facebook founder, hitting refresh like the rest of us, it really put things in perspective.

Does she like me? Does he love me? Does she want me? Does he care? Am I interesting? In a thousand ways, you and I chase validation, begging the world to respond to us, to friend us, to make us feel significant and seen. We measure our self-worth in terms of virtual friends and think "likes" are the key to success, even as the world's assessment of us is fleeting, and both in its commendation of us and in its contempt for us, we can never be sure where we stand. I love the way gospel hip-hop artist Lecrae communicated the raw reality of this truth on Twitter: "If you live for people's acceptance, you'll die from their rejection." There's a lot of truth to that.

When we allow others' opinions of us to determine our value, we're either driven to overconfidence or outright despair. The people we know say we're awesome, we're funny, we're talented, we're cool, and we soar on cloud nine for days and days, believing the inflated posts we write about ourselves.

No matter what platform we use, the same people who liked us last week turn on us and hate on us, casting us aside like yesterday's trash, and we plummet from the highest high to the lowest low, believing nobody likes us, nobody loves us, nobody cares. Self-harm always traces back to this soul-numbing sense that our lives are worthless and that we don't count.

Theologian or Thief: Who's Right with God?

One time there were two men who went up to the temple to pray. One of them was a church leader, a guy who knew the ins and outs of religion. In a setting like a temple, this guy fit in. On the outside, he had it all together. His clothes were spotless and ironed with starch. His hair was well groomed without giving the impression he was trying hard to look nice. He looked right, he said the right things, he practiced the right rituals, and he was good at what he did. He was humble and very proud of it! And yet Jesus would have a few choice words for him.

The other character in the story was a social outcast. The Scriptures say he was a tax collector, which in biblical times was about as shady as it gets. Think Robin Hood, except the opposite. Tax collectors would rob the poor and give to . . . themselves. If I were to equate it to negative modern-day reputations, think Wall Street greed meets armed robbery. Tax collectors in Jesus' day were self-seeking opportunists who bent the rules in order to exploit people who were already penniless, scraping by. They were hated and feared. And yet this man, this horrible excuse for a human being, was entering the temple to pray.

So, here they both are, the theologian and the thief, I'll call them, separated only by a few wooden pews. And now they're about to pray. In Jesus' story, we're invited to eavesdrop on the theologian's prayer first.

"Oh, God," the theologian says, his voice booming like one of those superstar television preachers for anyone and everyone to hear. "I thank you that I am not like other people—robbers, crooks, adulterers, or, heaven forbid, like this tax man. I fast twice a week and tithe on all my income" (Luke 18:11).

I like to picture this theologian, standing there in his church robes and official head covering, his sparkling résumé reflecting the sunlight filtering in through the narrow windows lining the wall, with his arms bent at ninety degrees, his palms flipped up toward the heavens, his Duck Dynasty beard rising and falling with each bombastic syllable that emerges from his lips. I imagine his head tilted back a little, his brow furrowed in seriousness, his eyes of course shut tight at the perfect pressure of spirituality. And as the words come out, slow and punctuated by meaningful pauses, I see him nodding in agreement with himself—"Wow. That was good. Can we get a recording of that? You can get your copy in the back. I am awesome." The whole thing is for show. It's the religious spirit, through and through.

Across the room is the thief, and he too has come ready to pray. But the response to his prayer is far different. While the theologian's performance evokes a standing ovation, the very presence of the thief has everyone in attendance glaring in disbelief. "How does he dare show himself here?" they grumble, their reaction to him overt and harsh. Various translations of the Bible say that the man was slumped in the shadows, standing at a distance with his face in his hands, not daring to raise his eyes toward heaven. He was so convicted that he wouldn't even look up to God. With his face buried, he was striking his chest, rocking back and forth on his heels, as tears streamed down his face. I picture him eventually folding himself down to the floor, unashamedly lifting up cries of remorse.

The Amplified Bible says that his actions were born of humility and repentance, that the reason he was so moved in those moments was because he'd encountered the presence of God. The words he prayed support that idea: "God, be merciful and gracious to me, the [especially wicked] sinner [that I am]!" (Luke 18:13, AMP). He was in essence saying, "I'm a total mess here, undeserving of any good thing. I have no hope except you, God. I've come to the end of myself."

Both men left the temple that day, but only one of them left "right with God," the Bible says. "If you walk around with your nose in the air, you're going to end up flat on your face," the story concludes. "But if you're content to simply be yourself, you will become more than yourself" (Luke 18:14). Now, if only we knew how to be ourselves. Who are we, really, anyway?

Who We Really Are

The reason so many of us struggle with self-image issues is that we fail to define ourselves in light of God. And yet that's exactly what the Scriptures say we must do, if we're ever to get a truthful take on who we are. "The only accurate way to understand ourselves," Romans 12:3 says, "is by what God is and by what he does for us, not by what we are and what we do for him."

Something inside of me protests, "Look at me! I'm cool, aren't I? Look at my likes, all my awesome pictures, my amazing fashion sense, my genius sense of humor—don't any of these things count at all?" I spent time with a pastor friend of mine in New York City last week, and this topic of self-image came up. He said, "Nick, the more people I talk to, the more I realize we're far more interested in imitation than revelation. We spend an inordinate amount of time and energy comparing ourselves with celebrities, with our friends, with anything that moves and breathes. If we invested even a fraction of those things in seeking divine revelation, we'd be far happier as a people and a whole lot healthier too." To his point, seek revelation over imitation.

It is tempting to turn to instant gratification instead of eternal satisfaction. It's tempting, isn't it, to lean on the things we can do, the people we can attract, the witty tweets we can post, the deals we can swing to get life to go the way we think it should go, instead of leaning on the sufficiency of God? But in the end, he's the only thing—the only One—who can bear our full weight. The other stuff may momentarily puff us up during the monotony of our days, but in the end it always deflates under the burdens of real life.

The annoying, boastful theologian who is posing as he prays? That's not who he really is. He is a chosen son of God, destined to be full of mercy, kindness, and gentleness (see Romans 8:33, Colossians 3:12).

The guy Facebook-stalking in desperate search of a coveted "friend"? That's not who he really is. He is a man created to live a life firmly rooted, built up, established in his faith, and overflowing with gratitude and the sense of being greatly loved by God (see Colossians 2:7, Romans 1:7, Ephesians 2:4, 1 Thessalonians 1:4).

The girl named Michelle you met in chapter 1, the one who had been cutting up her skin for five long years, wishing she could just die? That's not who she really is. She is a creation of the Most High, alive to God, a believer who has the light of the gospel shining in her mind (see Romans 6:11, 1 Thessalonians 5:23, 2 Corinthians 4:4).

Since we're talking about self-esteem, I'd like to dispel any notion that I'm somehow immune to what everyone else struggles with. For years—at least since I was a teenager—I've battled depression. There have been weeks when I didn't want to participate in the day and times when negative thoughts have crept into my mind and made me question who I am, what I'm doing with my life, and whether my efforts matter at all. Sometimes those periods are brought on by exhaustion or emotional depletion, and sometimes it seems like an all-out spiritual attack. No matter the cause, I know that I hate feeling depressed. I hate being down. I hate feeling tired at the simple thought of taking on a day. When our self-esteem takes a hit, it seems to impact every other area of our lives. And that's why this topic is so important.

When we struggle with our self-esteem, there is a great temptation to distract ourselves from what is really going on. Rather than checking the gauges and realizing we are running low in some area of our lives, we try to cope. Whether it's with friends, fun, flings, substance abuse, social media, self-harm, work, or Netflix, the things we turn to seem so gratifying in the moment. But the truth is that we will never find satisfaction without going to the Source. Deep down, we know better than to look to these things to pull us out of a funk, but there are always the same instant fixes within reach. I talk to people all the time who keep struggling with the exact same thing over the exact same issue, often at exactly the same time. Temptation is actually quite predictable, when we open our eyes to it. And yet we run toward the same vices again and again, hoping that this time they'll make good on their promises, that this time, they'll soothe our souls.

Of course they never do. By grace alone, we are welcomed back to our Father.

God reminds me that when I'm down and out and an emotional wreck, the guy who is down and out and an emotional wreck isn't really who I am. I am a new creation in Christ (2 Corinthians 5:17). I am empowered by the knowledge and glory of God (2 Peter 1:3–4). I've been delivered from the grip of darkness and adopted into God's eternal kingdom (Colossians 1:13). I have been strengthened with all power according to God's glorious might (Colossians 1:11). I have a spirit not of fear and depression and angst, but of power, and of love, and of a sound mind (2 Timothy 1:7).

And the same is true for you. Whatever dark thoughts lurk in the recesses of your mind, convincing you that you're not smart, that you're not compassionate, that you're not important, that you're not enough—those beliefs can be silenced as we start taking God at his word and clinging to his promises for our life. The lies of hell cannot stand when we declare the name of Jesus. The truth about you is that you are created in the image of God to be holy and blameless before him. You were designed to have the mind of Christ and the peace of God pulsing through your veins. You were built to house the living God, the One who has overcome all things, including death itself. And that presence, the Holy Spirit of God, dwells inside you because of Jesus' sacrifice on the cross. Your debt has been paid in full.

If you were sitting with me right now, I'd want to encourage you with how much God loves you. He loves you so much. Someone once told me that whenever I feel like I'm a hundred miles away from God, God is actually right there, one step in the other direction. Our job is simply to stop running and turn to him. Nineteenth-century British poet Francis Thompson called God the Hound of Heaven, meant to imply that even when we run from him, he is actively chasing us down.

At the close of each of the poem's sections, after Thompson describes his failed attempts to flee, God—the Hound of Heaven himself—speaks. In essence, he says that if we betray God, we'll be betrayed by everything else we try to install in our lives in his place. If we refuse to allow God to make his home in our minds and hearts and bodies, then we will never find shelter for ourselves. If we refuse to find contentment in Jesus, we'll never truly be content.

The poem's final lines read this way, with God speaking:

> Ah, fondest, blindest, weakest,
> I am He Whom thou seekest.[35]

He knows we'll never find our self-value, our self-worth, in the things of this world, and so Jesus comes on a rescue mission for us, eagerly hoping we'll turn from our brokenness and call on him. He knows exactly what we are looking for and offers himself fully. It's only in him that we can be wise. It's only in him that we find understanding. It's only in him that revelation is ours.

Scripture tells us that we're his workmanship, literally formed in the image of God and created in Christ Jesus to do good works. As we trust the great Hound of Heaven, we are forgiven and redeemed. As God's children, we are royalty and among those who reflect the very light of heaven. In Jesus, we have power over our enemy, and by his Spirit we are equipped with everything we will ever need. By Jesus' name, we are healed so that we can go heal others. This is who we really are. God's children. Healed. Redeemed. Reset and on mission to tell the world about the only one who saves—Jesus.

Humility Versus Self-Harm

Going back to my illustration of the theologian and the thief, let me ask you a question. Assuming that the theologian (or religious leader) had maintained his prideful and judgmental approach to life, never recognizing that every gift he had was not from himself but from above, what do you suppose would have become of him in the end?

The outcome is all too predictable; we see it all the time. Those who live their lives only for their money, their fame, their religious status, or their pride all end up the same: bitter and all alone. When we build our lives on sinking sand, it has a tendency to sink us. By making life all about us, we drive everyone else away. In our efforts to be admired by all, we are admired by none. Pride lies to us. It leads people from all walks of life away from logic and into some insane notion that we can stand next to Mount Everest and say, "I'm tall."

Really? You're tall? Even if you were six foot six, what is that compared to Everest at *thirty thousand feet* high. People *die* trying to climb that thing. They need supplemental oxygen just to *survive.*

Only fools stand beside a mountain and think they are tall. Wisdom and humility admits that we do not measure up. That's why the thief's posture was elevated in the story, the posture that says, "God, I'm the opposite of tall here. I'm desperate. Please, please intervene."

Let me be clear that if the thief had clung to his despair—that he was a mess, that he was hopeless, that he was sinking into despair—and chosen to cope with some vice rather than turning to God, he would have been every bit as guilty as the other man. And ultimately just as alone. Whether we're placing our hope in our accomplishments or some overt form of self-harm, until we surrender to Jesus, we're all guilty of injury to self. We don't need to have a blade to our wrist or lighter to our thigh to be a candidate for self-harm. Every time we turn to something other than Jesus, we're only hurting ourselves.

In Mark 4, there's an intense story that unfolds as Jesus is teaching his disciples next to the sea. After the morning lesson, Jesus tells his friends he wants to head to the other side of the sea. So they board a boat and set off to the other side, and Jesus curls up for a nap in the stern of the boat. As the story goes, they barely get beyond the horizon when a massive storm erupts and the disciples panic. It's important to note here that many of the disciples were seasoned fishermen, which means this storm must have been something crazy huge to scare these guys! So after trying their best to make it across the sea, they are left with no other solution than to wake up Jesus. Whether they were waking him so he could give a final blessing as they sunk collectively or whether they thought he could do something about it, we don't know. But after pulling the sleep from his eyes, Jesus does the most bizarre thing any of them have ever seen. He stands up and shouts across the raging sea. "Quiet!" he says. "Settle down!" (Mark 4:39). And then he looks back at his disciples, mumbles some frustrated words over having been wakened, and drifts back to sleep.

Jesus' buddies are floored. "Wait. What just happened?" He was sleeping . . . we were about to be shark bait . . . then he was awake and yelling at the water . . . and it listened . . . and now he's napping again?! If social media had existed, I guarantee you #JesusRocks would have been trending. They knew that Jesus was special, but what were they supposed to make of this? Even nature was at his beck and call, being silenced when he said to shut up.

As the group eventually reached the other side of the sea, the text says that Jesus got out of the boat and then things got nuttier still. You can read it for yourself in Mark 5, verses 1–20. A madman comes running toward Jesus from the cemetery where he lived. Yes, I said that he lived in a cemetery, which means we basically just flipped from *Deadliest Catch* right into an episode of *Walking Dead.* According to the story, this guy lived among the tombs because he was run out of town by people who didn't want to live next to the crazy dude.

Mark 5 says that no one could restrain this guy—he could not be stopped with rope or even chain. So we're talking about some kind of incredible zombie hulk here. And so day and night Zombie Hulk wanders among the graves and hills, screaming out and slashing himself with sharp stones.

While I don't know any zombie hulks for real, this story does remind me of a lot of the people I meet when I'm on the road, people whose situations have them totally locked up. They may not live in a literal cemetery, but their situations are equally dark. The insecurity and dysfunction they experience day after day after day drives them to think and do utterly unimaginable things. I met a young guy once who handed me a worn, crumpled, handwritten letter that he didn't want to keep anymore. It was a letter from his dad about what a worthless human being he, the son, was. This kid had hung on to and read that letter every day for years. Those awful words from his father had defined who he was. He was held captive by hate. He began cutting because he deserved nothing more than to be slashed and abused. He'd spent his life screaming inside, pleading with someone—anyone—for a way out.

I think it's why the madman in Mark 5 was screaming too.

As Jesus approached the man, the Bible says the man ran and bowed in worship before him. The evil spirit that had inhabited the man then warned Jesus not to mess with him. (Told you this story is crazy.) Incredibly, Jesus spoke back to the evil spirit. "Tell me your name," Jesus implored him, to which he said, "My name is Mob. I'm a rioting mob."

Mob then begged Jesus not to banish him from the country but instead to send him to the nearby herd of pigs to live inside them instead. (Apparently Mob liked bacon.)

So Jesus gave the order, and moments later, the madman was sane, the pigs were possessed, and the story of the zombie hulk and demonic bacon spread like a wildfire—check that: a *grease* fire—throughout the land.[36]

My point in all this: The same God who steadied the boat in the storm and who steadied the soul of a tormented man stands ready to steady us too. He has the power over the wind and waves. He has the power over every force of darkness. He has the power to set you free. If you are deceiving yourself by believing you're the bomb, open your ears to the steadying voice of Jesus in your life. And if you are deceiving yourself by believing you're worthless, reach out for the steadying hand of Jesus that is able to break your chains.

God is looking for people willing to simply come to him and admit their need. Humility is what he is after, and once we exhibit that, everything about our existence—our thoughts, our attitudes, our actions, our self-image—gets set fully and miraculously right. As Jesus speaks and we listen, our lives of chaos take on the calm of those who know whose hands they are in.

Humility at the feet of Jesus, or a lifetime of self-harm—these are the choices.

That praying thief discovered what I pray this generation will find, that there is nothing better than knowing God. There is no greater joy than to be in the house of the Lord forever, earnestly seeking him, honestly engaging him, fully depending on him, and believing every word of who he says we are. "The one thing I ask of the Lord," the psalmist David once wrote, "the thing I seek most—is to live in the house of the Lord all the days of my life, delighting in the Lord's perfections and meditating in his Temple" (Psalm 27:4, NLT).

If you ask God to increase in your life, he will always grant that request.

Ready for a Reset?

What Zuckerberg needed at the end of *The Social Network* wasn't a screen refresh. He needed a *soul* refresh, a resetting of that which is really real, which may be the very thing you are in need of today. If your self-image could use a tune-up, then let me offer up two straightforward starting points. First, come before God in a spirit of honesty and humility; and second, find a friend you can trust.

Shoot Straight with God

To reset your self-image, I suggest giving the thief's honest prayer a try. It may be the only time following a thief's example is a good idea. If you've been running from God, tell him. If you've been making choices you know aren't great, tell him. If you've been doubting your worth, tell him. If you're in need of his mercy, tell him. Be honest with God. You can't hide from him anyway, so why battle this life alone?

Ask God to open your eyes to who you are in him and to help you start believing that those things are actually true. He made you. He has plans and purposes for you. He has sought you, and he cares. Regardless of the madness your life has known, he is pursuing you even now.

To the boastful, he says, "Come."

To the bashful, he says, "Come."

To the confident, he says, "Come."

To the condemned, he says, "Come."

To you—whoever you are, wherever you've been, and whatever mistakes you've made—he says, "Child, please. Come."

You will never regret the time you spend looking to Jesus. This is why we keep coming into God's presence, shooting straight with him and inviting him to shift our perspective—of life, of him, and of ourselves.

Don't Go It Alone

Next, find someone who loves God, who loves you, and who will journey with you as these changes take place. In other words, seek out a friend or mentor who will remind you of who you are, whose you are, and God's potential and plans for your life.

The reason most of us wind up with a flawed self-image is that we've believed some lies along the way, and to get those lies untangled from your heart, you're going to need someone to speak truth into your life. You're going to need that friend who will look you in the eye and say, "You're trying to go it alone again. Quit striving. Let God in." You're going to need someone to pick you up after you've fallen down and tell you it's going to be okay.

In the midst of an enormously stressful season this past year, I decided to get a tattoo on my right forearm to be a daily reminder of who is in charge of my life. The tattoo reads, "The fight we're in has already been won,"[37] which is a Hillsong United lyric from their tune "Arise." When I see the words, I'm reminded that Jesus is on the throne and everything is going to be okay. I fight from a place of victory and not of defeat. Whatever battle I'm fighting—the battle to seem smart or cool or always put-together, the battle over my errant thoughts, the battle to believe there's a purpose for my life, and more—I know that Jesus has already won.

I don't know what your specific battle is, but I do know that in Jesus you've already won.

7

Jesus, Reset My Relationships

In the famous biblical story known as the parable of the prodigal son, I like to imagine that the son is named something like Jim. (The actual account is found in Luke 15:11–32, and I encourage you to read it in its entirety—mostly because my version, which follows, is a little . . . creative . . . you might say.)

When we meet Jim, he's living the life. His parents loved God and they loved Jim. They had invited him to become involved in the family business, and they were taking care of all his needs. On the outside, everything was great. But in Jim's inner world, a battle raged. At school and on his smartphone, Jim was being exposed to a life that seemed more exciting than the monotony he knew. Were his parents causing him to miss out? He began to question whether he wanted to stay home and whether his parents' rules were best for him. After weeks of negative peer pressure and a growing sense of bitterness, he went up to his mom and dad and said, "I hate your rules, and I hate you. I wish you were dead, because then I could get my inheritance and get out of here."

Now, I don't know how your parents would have responded to those sentiments, but Jim's parents said, "Okay, son. If that's what you want, then we'll go ahead and give you your inheritance now." And with a fat wad of cash in his pocket, Jim took off.

Celebrity culture—and music especially—has a lot to say about what will make us happy. Fergie says you have to be glamorous,[38] Nickelback says you have to be a rock star,[39] and Usher says you just need to party a little more.[40] Like many before him, Jim bought into the message and thought he'd give that path a try. He landed in Vegas and decided to live it up, banking on the adage being true that what happens in Vegas really does stay in Vegas. Jim got a penthouse suite at the Bellagio, bumped along the Strip in a Land Rover with spinner rims, and poured all his energies into partying like a rock star. Sex, drugs, rock and roll . . . and all-you-can-eat buffets. This was the *life,* Jim thought.

Relationship Matters

A few years after PULSE started, a pastor named Mike Montgomery called me and said, "Nick, I want to invest in your life. I believe that God has called you to tell millions in your generation about Jesus, and I want to help you stay the course." I had no way of knowing just how impactful that call would be. Mike had heard about PULSE, and about me, and wanted to know if he could serve as a sounding board while I got the ministry on its feet. Mike had no way of knowing that at the same time he was reaching out to me, I was asking God for a mentor. I prayed for a godly, more mature man whom I could bounce ideas off of, someone who could help me prioritize my life, a friend who had already walked the path I found myself on and who had stayed out of the ditch along the way.

That was more than eight years ago, and throughout all the twists and turns I've experienced, Mike has been with me, as near as a phone call or a text.

Just two weeks ago, I was stressed out and feeling anxious while on the road. I was in Nashville for some meetings, and it was ten o'clock at night when I finally decided I needed to phone Mike. I halfway hoped he wouldn't pick up—I didn't want to interrupt his family time or freak him out, given the late hour. But when he did pick up and I heard his calming voice, I had a sigh of relief. "Hey, Nick!" he said in his enthusiastic way. "How's it going? I've been praying for you!"

Mike and I caught up for the first few minutes of the call, but then there was that long pause that told him there was a deeper reason I'd reached out. I told Mike that I felt like I'd been pushing lately, that I'd been running so hard that I felt worn out physically, emotionally—even spiritually. The word that kept coming to mind as I talked with Mike was "striving." In our efforts to plan for the gathering on the National Mall for Together 2016, I'd been relentless in my pursuit of more meetings, more partnerships, more systems created to follow up with those who would surrender their lives to Jesus, and on and on it went. In short, I was falling into the trap of believing it all rested on my shoulders. I knew that striving wasn't something God encouraged in the Bible, and I knew that if I did not get this spirit of striving subdued in me, it would eat me alive.

Mike wasted no time on the heels of my explanation. "Let me pray for you," he said and then did. "Listen, if you don't last, Nick, this whole thing—God's call on your life, the mission he has you on, all your hard work to this point—it's all for nothing. I'd like to work with you on revising your schedule so that you feel at peace with your days and weeks instead of feeling enslaved to them."

We talked for a few minutes more, and then Mike suggested that I clear my calendar for two days upon returning home from the road and take Tiffany on a minivacation. He knew that I was feeling adrift at sea and that reconnecting with what was most important to me—Tiffany tops that list, second only to Jesus—would be the quickest way to re-anchor my soul. I flew home the next day, repacked a bag, and took Tiffany to a cabin in northern Minnesota. Mike was right: the time away rebuilt something that had been torn down in my inner person. We all need a friend like Mike.

The Reason We Relate

When I was growing up, I thought of friends in terms of having fun, being popular, and hanging out. Friends related more to status than substance back then, but as I get older, I realize there is a much bigger purpose for my relationships—the connections I have to friends, mentors, family members, my wife, and others. At this point in my life I don't need more acquaintances. I need more "4 a.m. friends," as my friend Dave calls them—someone I can call at any hour, one who is always there for me. The most valuable people in my life are the ones who are loyal when things get hard, who tell me the truth even when it hurts, and who help me become the best version of me I can be. A true friend cares less about helping me feel better and more about calling me to what is better. Not all relationships can fit this bill, of course; there are people in my life who are friends only in the loosest meaning of the word—and that's completely fine. I don't need to bear my soul to Amad, who cuts my hair, or to Stacey, who serves me coffee at Starbucks. But to have a small circle of trusted loved ones who have my back, who shoot straight, and who readily engage in conversation about stuff that truly matters—that relational landscape is one everyone ought to pursue.

While I'm sure that Jesus was pretty self-sufficient (being God and all), he modeled for us that rather than going it alone in life, there ought to be a select group of people we rally to our side for deeper relationship. Friends encourage and challenge each other, creating a beautiful give-and-take that honors one another, while ultimately pointing to Jesus. Intentional friendship is one of the most powerful forces on earth, and we do well to seek relationships in this manner. There is nothing quite like true friendship. Accepting others, sharing Jesus with others, knowing others, loving others, serving others, helping others, being devoted to others, living at peace with others, maintaining harmony with others, instructing others, eating with others, being patient and kind with others, forgiving others, speaking highly of others, encouraging others, and considering others' needs before we consider our own.[41] Jesus himself modeled this dynamic for us in drawing three of his disciples—Peter, James, and John—closest to his side. They were his best friends, the men he spent the most time with and was most vulnerable with.

At PULSE I have an inner circle with Justin, Chris, Mike, and Jay. Not only do I work with these guys, but they are some of my best friends and I know they have my back. On Tuesdays I meet with my close friend Sammy, a fellow evangelist who sharpens me as we do accountability and pour into each other's lives. Within my family, I try to call my dad weekly, because I so deeply respect his voice in my life. Tiffany and I have a date night each week to stay connected and in tune with one another. My point: If you were to look at my calendar, you would see that my entire routine revolves around relationships. When we meaningfully and intimately engage with a few people in our own lives, we reflect Jesus to them, and any time spent reflecting Jesus is time really well spent.

I know many who simply refuse to sign up for this kind of life. Letting others in takes time and investment, and it reveals that we are vulnerable. Many prefer to cling to the illusion that they don't need anyone else. "It's easier this way. I'm not weak like those people. I like my life my way." We call these people loners (or worse), and the sad reality is that after enough time denying real friendship, no one wants to be their friend anyway. Even so, Jesus never sees a person un-friendable; he simply sees things as they truly are. And what he sees—that we often fail to take in—is that without meaningful relationships, we are community starved, never knowing the beauty of a relationship that is working right. This is why he calls us into active community. He tells us to reach out to the loners and surround them with love and grace. It's why he tells us to look like him and speak like him and act like him so that everyone can know the joy of fitting in and the feeling of true community. This is the good news of the gospel at its core: everyone has been welcomed into a great big family, where the only requirement for admission is acknowledging that they can't go it alone. We all need a Rescuer. We all need a Savior. We all need Jesus. And we all need each other. Standing equal at the cross, Christian community can change everything.

So, while surface-level conversations are fine, the majority of our relational energy should be spent with people who are on the journey toward becoming like Jesus. This is why we prioritize participating with a local church, getting involved in a small group, meeting with other believers for prayer, and sitting across a table with a few people and enjoying a meal and talking about what counts. In other words, we don't connect with a faith community in order to please our parents or pass some celestial test. We connect with a faith community because it's undeniably good for our soul.

What to Look for in a Friend

Just after my fifth birthday, I ran away from home. Or that's what I called it, anyway. More specifically, that's what my buddy Todd called it. According to the calendar, Todd was only a few years older than I was, but in terms of street smarts, he had lapped me several times. Todd was one of the handful of neighborhood boys I played with regularly during my early childhood, and while he was my favorite friend, my mom was always worried when we hung out. "When you two are together, you seem to get in a lot of trouble," I remember her saying.

Looking back, I can see that maybe Todd and I weren't the best influence on each other, even as I utterly idolized him way back then. He was a few years older, and everything Todd did was fun. It was exciting. Risky. Bold. When I was with Todd, I got to act like a big kid. Todd and I would regularly sneak past the geographical boundaries my mom had set for me—"Nick, you may not ride your bike past the Nelsons' house"—and I would get to throw rocks at squirrels and listen to them squeal in horror as Todd and I cackled and ran off.

For the record, running away that day was Todd's idea, despite the fact that I jumped at the chance to tag along. One afternoon when my siblings and I were supposed to be napping, I crept out of my bedroom, across the living room, and right on through the front door. My sleep-deprived mom had fallen asleep with my brother, Billy, who was a baby at the time, so I figured I had a good hour or so to play outside before I needed to sneak back into my room.

When I hit the front porch, I found Todd in our front yard, hanging out. "Nick!" he said, a glimmer of mischief in his eye. "You wanna run away?"

I reflexively grinned. "Run away?" I asked. "Sure! That sounds great! What does it mean?"

In a matter of moments, our plan was hatched. We would run away, right then, right there, coming back home who knows when. It was all very scandalous and exciting.

Todd and I grabbed our bikes and took off a full two blocks away, to the home of one of Todd's relatives. "We did it!" Todd said. "We ran away!" I wasn't sure what running away typically equated to, but something in me knew we hadn't gone far. Todd knew where they had a spare key, which meant that not only had we run away, but also we had broken into a home. This was getting more exciting by the minute. Inside the home were pet gerbils and a basement of toys I had yet to conquer. Bliss.

Time passed—two hours maybe?—and then Todd's relatives returned home. After registering the full shock of finding two unattended youngsters in their home, messing with all their stuff à la Goldilocks, they warned Todd and me that they'd have to tell our parents what we'd done. Todd and I sat on the step outside and waited in agony for our moms to arrive. It was the early-childhood equivalent of waiting on death row for justice to be served. When my own mother pulled up, she was sobbing—not sad tears, but mad. I didn't like mad tears at all.

Like most parents, mom had heard her share of news reports about children getting kidnapped, snatched right off safe neighborhood streets. I could hear mom's voice, "See? That could have been you."

After that little escapade, I think our moms collaborated so that Todd and I wouldn't hang out as much. In all honesty, it was probably for the better. It's like the index card that had been taped to my bathroom mirror for so long that its edges were beginning to curl; in my mom's scribbled handwriting it said, "Walk with the wise and become wise, for a companion of fools suffers harm. —Proverbs 13:20 [NIV]."

We both needed a wiser influence than either of us was providing.

What my mom intrinsically understood was something that would take me many more years to sort out: in the same way that plants require the right conditions in order to flourish—sunlight, water, nutrient-dense soil, a little space—people need certain elements in order to grow. Elements that don't look, sound, or act like two mischievous little boys, I should add.

If I hoped to grow as a young man and also as an early follower of Christ, I would need to surround myself with others who were growing in their relationship with Jesus too—and hopefully at a quicker clip than I was. That singular lesson would come into play during every major stage of development in my life, and it schools me still today: to become wise, we need to surround ourselves with people of wisdom.

I was in Iowa a few years ago and struck up a conversation with a group of teens about Jesus. As we talked, one of the guys in the group shared authoritatively that Jesus was a great doctor and how God was Jesus' son. I thought I misheard him: "Wait. God is Jesus' son?" I asked, to which he said, "Yeah, man, like I said."

Um. No. God is not Jesus' son. While I was trying to be gracious, I didn't know whether to be more shocked over the biblical ignorance of this young man or over the collective head nods of the other kids listening to him. It was clear that he was the group's expert on all things religion, which was more than a little disconcerting to me.

After taking the group through a brief history lesson, I reiterated the importance of going to the source for yourself. I could also have said a few things about who you should anoint as an expert in your life. Be sure the people you're learning from actually have something wise to teach. For example, when Mike told me that I needed to bag the rest of my plans and take my wife out of town, my initial (but thankfully silent) reaction was to scoff. I had way too much to get done and not nearly enough time to do it. Didn't Mike understand that part of the reason why I was calling him was precisely because I was having trouble getting everything done? Didn't he know that blowing off my responsibilities would make things worse, not better?

And yet the reason Mike is in my life is because he does understand. He has experienced or at least seen many situations like mine before. He knows me. He loves me. And he's committed to helping me grow. Which is why he suggested the course of action that he did; the only way I was going to grow last week was to push pause on all the madness and choose to simply rest.

The other elements that spurred my growth over the years have included prayer, confession, worship, and more, all of which we'll take a closer look at in chapter 9, on habits. But this idea of scrutinizing who I hang out with—and why—would prove to be the biggest game changer of them all.

When You're with Pigs, Wishing for Slop

Let's go back to Jesus' story about Jim. For a while, Jim was having fun, living like a cast member in his own music video. But unfortunately, somebody forget to tell him that music videos rely a lot on smoke and mirrors. As the smoke faded for Jim, his money was gone. And when the money ran out, the friends and women ran out with it. Jim lost everything as quickly as he'd found it, leaving him penniless, hopeless, and hung over.

It took Jim hitting rock bottom before he realized what he had back home. In Jesus' story, Jim finally does return home to his parents, where he is welcomed with open arms. Life begins to turn around for him, and everything works out in the end. But let me take you back to that scene where Jim is destitute and distressed and in need of a faithful friend. Can you imagine how Jim's life could have looked different if he'd had some people speaking truth into his life? "Hey, Jim," they might have said, "your family is actually pretty cool." Or, "Hey, Jim, you might want to take it easy with the crab legs." Or, "Jimmy-boy, I ain't saying she's a gold digger or anything, but come on, man!" Or, "Jim, tequila works better as a song than as a replacement for water." Or, "Jim, have you heard of a savings account . . . or church?"

Whenever I talk with people about the importance of seeking out relationships with wise people, the majority of the time, they look at me like I've grown a third eye. They know they're making foolish choices. They know they need wise friends. But when you're living like a fool, you tend to be surrounded by—any guesses? Fools. The Bible says that Jim was so broke and desperate that he had to take a job feeding pigs for a farmer who lived nearby. Jim would watch those pigs eating their slop, thinking, *Boy, that sure looks good.* Can you imagine being that hungry?

For Jim, something had to give. But where does a guy find a wise person to help him when he's spending his time with a bunch of pigs? Jesus said that finally Jim came to his senses, which is an impressive move for any wayward guy or girl, given how many people simply give up. He came to his senses, he opened his eyes, and he realized he needed to head home. For Jim, home is where wisdom was located, and so home is where he would go.

I hope it doesn't take you getting to that point of despair before your eyes are opened. I hope you'll make friends with wisdom today. The first step is a straightforward one; it's simply getting closer to someone who is wise.

Whenever I talk with someone who is done with living like a fool and who is ready to start living like the wise, I ask them this question: "Is there anyone in your life—a parent, an aunt or uncle, a coach, a neighbor, a colleague at work—who knows Jesus and who would be willing to help you in your journey from foolishness to wisdom, from death to life, from cynicism to faith?" For Jim, the answer was his parents. Who is it, I wonder, for you?

After an event in Kansas City a couple of years ago, a teenage girl named Allison who had responded to the gospel reached out to ask me how she could start growing in her faith. I asked her if she had a family member or a close friend who knew the Lord and could help her, and in response, she said, "No." I was skeptical. "Really?" I said. "Nobody? No spiritual grandma? No boss at work who talks about her church involvement? No big brother who has it together? No one?" Still, she said no. There was no one. No one who loved God, loved her, and was willing to help her grow.

I'd come across this issue before, which is why awhile back our team at PULSE created a system for helping people find their someone—someone somewhere who could help inspire their sin-scarred soul. We started by asking event attendees to text "RESET" to the number 73738. Once we received the text, we then sent that person a link to digital devotions, day-by-day encouragement that would help kick-start their walk with Jesus. If they wanted to connect with someone else, we offered a phone number and point of connection to a digital counselor. We also began to ask the person to send in the phone numbers of one or two Jesus followers who might be willing to help him or her grow, and then we would text the same digital devos to those supporters so that they could walk through the material with the person who had responded to Jesus.

For Allison, even though initially she couldn't think of a single person who could help her, after a few exchanges with our team, she said, "Wait! I do know a Christian. But he's only a Facebook friend. And he lives in Alaska."

Typically, we encourage guys to seek out guys and girls to seek out girls, and we tell people to think of supports who live close by, but given the lack of support system this girl had, we decided a Facebook friend in Alaska would have to do. It turns out the guy was a seminary student and wasn't just willing to help out; he was honored to do so. He received the devotions each week and patiently walked through the content with Allison, and over time, she did mature.

Each week, Allison printed out the devotions too—on the printer at work. One day, her coworker happened by the printer and found the devotion lying on the tray. Employees weren't supposed to use company equipment for personal projects (the topic of honesty hadn't yet been addressed in the Bible study), but as this coworker headed off to find Allison, she started reading the devotion she'd picked up off the printer tray. And she was compelled by what she read.

When she found Allison, she said, "I was coming over here to remind you not to use the printer for personal reasons, but now I have a bigger question for you. Can you forward me this? Are there more like this one I can have?"

That coworker surrendered her life to Jesus, and Allison wound up being her supporter.

My point here is that everyone has to start somewhere, and it's far easier to make it when we include others in our journey. Everyone who comes to Jesus would benefit from someone who is farther along on the spiritual journey and who can show him or her what it means to love God with your whole passion and with your prayers and with your muscle and with your intelligence (Luke 10:27). We all need a faithful (and faith-filled) friend.

What's After Awkward

I've talked to dozens of people who think of a supporter or two and are ready to reach out but get stuck in the anticipation of it feeling really, really awkward. And for good reason: talking about Jesus seems a little . . . weird. We don't know what to say. We don't know how to say it. And the emotional paralysis we feel seems impossible to overcome. In the midst of these realities, here's my advice to you: start with the four simple words, *Can we get together?*

That's it: "Can we get together?"

If the people you're making the request of are mature and godly (which, as we've discussed, they should be), then you've got nothing to worry about. They'll probably respond with some version of, "Absolutely. What's on your mind?"

To that one, just say, "I've been thinking about my life and about what really matters. I'm trying to seek out a few people who will have a good influence on me. That's why I reached out to you."

If the person is an existing friend, then modify your words slightly to something along these lines: "I know we've been friends for a while, but we've never really talked about God—or about anything that matters. I'd like to do that, if you're open to it."

Secure a time and place to meet. And then don't let anything out-prioritize that meeting. Keep your commitment. Pray and show up on time. Share what's on your heart. And prepare for God to do cool things as a result.

When we welcome Jesus into our friendships, everything changes.

I will tell you that during that first time with your supporter, it will be easier to talk about almost anything other than Jesus. It just will. You'll be tempted to chat about the crazy rainstorm that erupted on your way to the coffee shop, or how your dog wouldn't stop barking at 5 a.m., or how you got tickets to whatever concert is coming to town that month, or how your team really blew it in last night's game. A little chitchat is fine, but don't dwell there. Something radical happens when God is invited into our relationships, and I would hate for you to invest a couple of hours with another person and never reap the rewards of going deep.

Yes, talking about Jesus those first few times will feel forced.

Yes, it will seem agonizingly awkward.

Yes, you will want to ditch the whole deal and go back to talking about Instagram or the new Bieber single.

But the reason all of this will be true is the same reason you desperately need these conversations in your life. You feel weird talking about spiritual matters because you haven't made a practice of talking about spiritual matters. And as a result, your friendships have been centered on things that aren't making the difference you need. Invite God in, and watch your life transform.

As I was graduating from high school and heading off to college and starting to sense God's call on my life, my cousin Tim died unexpectedly in a car accident. He was only in his twenties, and the jolt of that loss sent me reeling. At his funeral, I sat there with tears of regret streaming down my face. Here's what I regretted: I'd had countless conversations with Tim about all sorts of things—basketball and music and shoes and girls. But I'd never really talked to him about Jesus. I'd never told him about the most important part of my life, and now he was gone. Forever. Fortunately, I know that Tim had a faith of his own. But that day, I vowed that I would devote the rest of my life to telling people about Jesus—especially the people I say I love. I never wanted to feel that sense of regret again. The truth is, if I say we are friends and yet I haven't talked to you about Jesus, I'm not much of a friend. True friendship is based on selfless love. Love comes from the Father and without him, there is no love.

But with Jesus—right there in the midst of our everyday conversations—there is power. There is provision. There is healing. There is joy. When we usher whatever shame or darkness we've been wrestling with into the bright light of day, we find that wholeness and holiness have been waiting for us, ready to embrace us, ready to change us for the better, ready to give us fresh perspective, ready to make us wise. This is what Jim experienced when he finally returned home.

You've Been Healed to Help Others Get Healed

A benefit of facing the awkwardness of asking for help to grow in Jesus is that you do, in fact, grow in Jesus. And once you are sturdy and steady and able to see things from God's point of view, you can turn around and help rescue someone else who's going down. In the same way that Allison matured in her faith and was then able to encourage her colleague in the ways of Jesus, you too can be that warm, welcoming, nonjudging, loving, honest friend someone desperately needs. With God, nothing is wasted. The tests God has carried you through will become the testimony he uses in someone else's life. You can call out something beautiful in that struggling soul and remind that friend of who they are in Christ. You can answer their phone call and say, "Yes! I'd love to meet with you and help you grow. You don't have to feel ashamed with me. Trust me, I've been there too. I've walked through a lot of junk and a lot of pain, and I promise to shoot straight about it all. You tell me what you need, and I will do my best to be there for you. Now. Tell me what's going on . . ."

We have a simple approach we use at PULSE called Keep5. Once people surrender their lives to Jesus and start understanding what it looks like to live for him, we tell them to jot down a list of five people they know who would benefit from going God's way in life. They log the names in an app like Evernote or scribble them on a card to put in their Bible or on their fridge, and then each day they look at those names and say a prayer for each of those people, that God would do something miraculous in their lives. It's uncanny how many times one of those Keep5 people reaches out to the person who has been praying for them and says, "I can't explain what's going on in my heart, but I think it's God."

In Colossians 4:3, the apostle Paul, a dear friend of Jesus, tells us as believers not to forget to pray that "God will open doors for telling the mystery of Christ." Each time we pray for our Keep5 friends, we are doing just that; we are asking God to open a door of opportunity for our relationship with that person to go deeper, to include God, to count not only here on earth but for all eternity with Jesus. Those who incorporate this type of activity into their lives always wind up saying, "I thought partying was fun. Those days have nothing on this. I have a front row seat to lives being truly changed."

Ready for a Reset?

Take a minute to survey the relational landscape of your life. Do you see strong, tall oak trees surrounding you, or do you see a bunch of flimsy twigs being whipped about by the wind? If you are struggling to make wise decisions, then the first step you need to take is to solicit some real help. Here's where to begin.

Open Your Heart

After you assess the strength (or weakness) of your relational world, come before God with the truth. If you need increased wisdom, then ask God to bring someone who is wise into your life. As I mentioned earlier, once you start looking for something, you tend to find it. If you are looking for chaos and drama, you will find it. But if you are looking for sturdiness and sage counsel, you will find that instead. So, ask. Keep asking and keep looking, until you find someone who's wise.

Open Your Mouth

Next, refuse to cave to fear or insecurity as you contemplate reaching out. Simply contact the person or people you know can help you, muster the courage to drop them a line, and then make your bold request: "Can we get together?" Ask God to give you the words to say from there, and trust that he has good things in store for you, as you surround yourself with beauty and truth.

8

Jesus, Reset My Purity

If there is one area that those I've talked to have wanted to reset more than any other, it relates to purity. Most of us know what it feels like to cross the line, watch the video, give in to the temptation, and experience the shame of regret. Whether our issues are physical, mental, emotional, or all of the above, sometimes purity seems like a myth.

Based on the themes I've collected from more than half a million reset prayers (prayer requests sent in by PULSE event attendees), it's clear the longing to be made new is a universal one. A couple of years ago, published figures from the Centers for Disease Control and Prevention reported that of the high school students surveyed, half had had sexual intercourse, a third had had sex in the last three months, and about one in six had had sex with four or more people in their lifetime.[42] What they didn't report on were the emotions that accompany those stats. Kids feel ashamed, confused, used, embarrassed, violated, shattered, and vile. While we often believe the call to wait is God's desire to rob us of normal adolescent fun, in hindsight we realize it's actually his strategic plan for saving us vast amounts of agonizing pain, shame, and embarrassment from our decisions.

Between the physical sex acts they've engaged in and their participation in the fantasy worlds of explicit chat rooms and online porn—recent studies reveal that 70 to 80 percent of students have been exposed (either voluntarily or involuntarily) to pornographic imagery by age eighteen, and that the age of first exposure for boys could be as young as eight years old.[43] It seems that each year, I meet younger and younger kids who are struggling with issues that seem completely out of place for their age. It's like watching an entire generation robbed of its childhood—its innocence, its wholeness. In its place is a reality that no one should have to face.

On Being Dirty and Clean

During summers when I was in high school, my buddies and I worked in the sugar beet fields outside of Grafton, North Dakota, a town about two hours north of Fargo known for its crystal sugar. We would wake up before 6 a.m. (which for teenage guys was showing remarkable responsibility), arrive at the fields by 7:30 or 8, and get to work heading up and down the long, straight rows, pulling beets as fast as we could. We were paid by the row, and given my competitive spirit, I always wanted to hit as many rows as possible and more rows than anyone else working the fields.

These were experimental plots we were working, which meant the farmer was testing all sorts of different fertilizer to see which ones grew the best beets. This meant going up and down rows of these freshly sprouted beats to remove extras so there was only one beet per hand-length. My friends and I used to joke that we were probably going to grow a third arm or break out in oozing sores all over our bodies as a result of working those fields. Who knew what was in the uncertified dirt we were caked in every day? Certainly, we didn't. All we knew was that the job paid more money than we could have earned doing almost anything else, and so we were highly committed to the task.

If I started at 8 a.m. sharp, by exactly 8:15, I would be covered from head to toe in a fine layer of fertilizer dust. By five in the afternoon, the dust would be under my fingernails, in my nostrils, and seeping, it seemed, from my pores. I'd walk in the door upon returning home and, before even greeting another human being, head straight for the shower. As the warm water streamed over my head, down my back, and into the drain, it took a river of jet-black grime with it. Every single day, I would stand there soapy and wet and deeply satisfied by the sensation of going from dirty to clean.

When we talk about purity, it's this same feeling of dirty we all know about. Students line up and tell me how they wish they could be made clean. If only there were a shower somewhere that could wash away the grime on their souls. These students have seen too much and done too much and know the sort of pain that seems too much to bear. They're shadowed by their sinfulness and can't find a way of escape. Like Job looking at his brokenness before God and wondering how it is possible for one man to have so many troubles in life, all seems hopeless: "Even if I washed myself with soap and my hands with cleansing powder," the prophet wrote, "you would plunge me into a slime pit so that even my clothes would detest me" (Job 9:30–31, NIV).

Sinfulness or Submission

The reason the pain associated with charting our own course sexually is so real is that this type of sin is what Scripture refers to as a violation of ourselves. In 1 Corinthians 6:18 (NIV), Paul says to "flee from sexual immorality" and then offers up the reason why: "All other sins a person commits are outside the body, but whoever sins sexually, sins against their own body."

Instinctively, we recognize this reality, even as we stand by the claim that sin is fun. As I've said before, sin is fun in the moment, which is why we are so slow to give it up. We keep trying to reconcile the momentary fun with the longer-term pain, but it never quite gets sorted out. And so we distract ourselves from facing the pain that is always right there, right at the surface of our consciousness. We distract ourselves with busyness. Or drunkenness. Or the facade of apathy. Or saying we're sorry and swearing we'll change, even as we know we never will. This pathetic progression—sinning again because I loved my sin, hating the feeling of having sinned again, swearing I'd do better next time, falling and failing and sinning again . . . all because I loved my sin—is exactly what I signed up for at age fourteen when I allowed a porn habit to capture my mind. This was happening while I was supposedly a follower of Jesus, mind you. I knew that I couldn't look at pornography and follow Jesus in the same moment, but the battle that raged inside of me over who would win out my hours was one I didn't want to fight. I wanted Jesus. And I wanted my sin. Something had to give.

In the midst of sin, God always seems distant, which makes perfect sense. During my teen years, I'd placed my brokenness and fallenness between me and God. And like the prophet Isaiah promised, that kind of prioritization always yields perilous results. "GOD's arm is not amputated," Isaiah wrote. "He can still save. GOD's ears are not stopped up—he can still hear. There's nothing wrong with God; the wrong is in *you.* Your wrongheaded lives caused the split between you and God. Your sins got between you so that he doesn't hear" (59:1–2).

The years have given me some perspective on that struggle I faced as a teen, and what I can see plainly now that I couldn't perceive back then was that God was waiting for me to hand over to him my memories and my mistakes, my habits and longings, all the deception and deviance, the full weight of all my sin. His arm was still long enough to save me, and his ears were still inclined toward the cries of my heart. He stood ready to offer me full forgiveness and complete freedom, but I had to be willing to let go of the grip I had on my sin. I needed to grip his hand instead.

When God surveys all the brokenness in our lives—the lying, the cheating, the swearing, the judgment, the gossip, the sleeping around—he is faced with a dilemma. He loves us and wants us to be happy, but like any good parent can see, sometimes allowing short-term pain is best for us in order for us to discover where real contentment is found. When we sin, we are choosing something other than God's best. He knows this. Deep down, we know this. What remains to be seen is whether we will shift our grip. Will we surrender our way for his?

Shifting Our Grip

In John 8, we meet a woman stuck in sexual sin who is outed in front of the whole town. For the purpose of the story, let's call her Amanda. Evidently, Amanda had been caught sleeping with someone else's husband, and consequently the religious leaders of the day dragged her to the center of the town square and said to the crowd that quickly gathered, "This woman is a whore. She deserves to die."

Can you imagine the shame of that experience? You get caught doing something you don't want people to catch you doing, and your dirt is put on display for all to see. Imagine all of your friends, neighbors, and family members glaring at you, spitting on you, and taunting you. "You're nothing more than a slut," they say. "You're guilty, through and through."

Adding to the pain of Amanda's experience was the reality that every pastor in town gathered for this little shame party. Beyond them, Jesus himself was on the scene. If anyone deserved to judge Amanda for her actions, it was Jesus. She was clearly guilty, and he was clearly not.

In the story, the pastors reminded Jesus that according to the law, the crowd had the right to stone this woman—literally, as in pick up big rocks and pelt her with them until she died. I don't know for sure how Amanda felt about Jesus, but I have to imagine that as she watched big men stoop down and pick up big rocks, she was thinking, *God, if you're real, I hope you show up . . . and fast.*

The ringleaders of this whole encounter looked at Jesus and asked, "What should we do?"

They were waiting for the green light from Jesus, the signal that would give them permission to take this woman down. "Come on, Jesus!" I can hear them saying. "Let us at her! Surely you won't tolerate this kind of thing!"

Verses 6 through 8 describe what happened next. "Jesus bent down and wrote with his finger in the dirt," the text says. "[The religious leaders] kept at him, badgering him. He straightened up and said, 'The sinless one among you, go first: Throw the stone.' Bending down again, he wrote some more in the dirt."

While we'll never know this side of heaven what Jesus scribbled in the sand, we do know that on that day, Jesus stepped in and saved Amanda's life—in the same way he steps in to save ours. Verse 9 says the oldest leaders in the crowd put down their weapons of judgment first, which I love. It's easy to pass judgment in our youth, but the more mature we become, the more we realize that all of us are broken and are desperately in need of grace. The old-timers had a lot of life on them; they definitely knew the score.

After everyone had departed, Amanda was left all alone. Jesus looked at her and said, "Amanda, where are they? Does no one condemn you?" to which she said, "No one, Master."

"Neither do I," said Jesus. "Go on your way. From now on, don't sin" (verses 10–11).

This is an important and defining lesson about Jesus: No matter what you are guilty of, Jesus does not reject you. He isn't against you. He isn't blind to you in your point of need. On the contrary, Jesus sees you. He loves you. Jesus' mission never involved condemning the world; John 3:16–17 says as much. God sent his son not to condemn the world but to save it. The world condemns us. We condemn us. We condemn each other. But Jesus? He's decidedly anti-condemnation. In your school-assembly program, Jesus could be the poster child for anti-bullying, if ever there were one. Jesus stands up for the outcast, the marginalized, and says to everyone watching, "I'm with him. I'm with her." This ought to come as really good news for us. Whatever wrongs we've committed, Jesus is there with us and for us, his presence saving our lives.

"You're not condemned," he reminds us. "You're not destined for a sinful life. Go. Go in peace. Go and sin no more."

It's the shifting of the grip I was talking about, when we let go of our life of sin and move forward hand in hand with him. That day Amanda's life was reset.

"I came so they can have real and eternal life," he says in John 10:10, "more and better life than they ever dreamed of." We think we know how to secure "more and better life" for ourselves. I certainly thought I knew back when I was chasing after sinking sand instead of Jesus. And I've talked with hundreds if not thousands of guys who have fallen into the very same trap. *If I can just fill up on her texts, her words, her likes, her hips, her kiss,* they think, *then I'll be satisfied. Then I won't feel this deep ache.* But of course that sort of filling up doesn't yield fulfillment in the end. At best, it's all a glimpse of something greater, an arrow pointing us back to God. At worst, we are left exposed and alone like Amanda, desperate for someone to show us a better way. Only Jesus fills us up in the end.

Only Jesus never knew dirtiness.

Only Jesus lived a sin-free life.

Only Jesus loved perfectly.

Only Jesus can cleanse us from sin.

And so, the offer: His life for yours. His death for yours. His purity for your waywardness. His hope for your deflated heart. That pang you feel whenever you observe innocence and beauty in daily life—a newborn baby, a genuine act of kindness, a breathtaking sunset, a belly laugh—that reminder that you're not innocent anymore, that something pure has been taken from you that you can never, ever get back . . . Jesus says, "You can be pure again. Innocent again. I'm offering you a fresh start. A reset."

The cleaning-up process isn't as visible as hopping in a shower and watching the rivers of dirt wash away, but it's every bit as real. Because the moment we release our grip on our sinfulness and open our hand to his, he holds us tight and forgives us, and he empowers us to go. To go in peace. To go and sin no more.

Dead and Gone

A few years ago, Justin Timberlake and T.I. released a song called "Dead and Gone" that says, "I've been travelin' on this road too long just trying to find, my way back home . . ."[44]

I don't know if there was any kind of spiritual motivation behind those words when they wrote them, but the theology they reflect is sound. Like Amanda thrown there at the feet of Jesus, so many of us have been walking on the road of impurity far too long, desperate to get back home to the way things used to be, to the way we used to be, to the innocence that used to be ours. As spectators, it's easy for us to comment to those who have been on the wrong road for too long, "Hey, maybe it's time to get on a different road!" But just like J.T. and T.I. say in the song, the only way to recapture the beauty is for the us that exists apart from God to be laid to rest, to be told, "You're dead and gone." Galatians 2:20 puts it this way: "I have been crucified with Christ. My ego is no longer central. It is no longer important that I appear righteous before you or have your good opinion, and I am no longer driven to impress God. Christ lives in me. The life you see me living is not 'mine,' but it is lived by faith in the Son of God, who loved me and gave himself for me. I am not going back on that."

The goal here is becoming a man or woman after God's own heart, because when we care more about staying connected to the heart of God than we do staying connected to our own selfish desires, we will find life that is truly life. This takes some real commitment, I'll grant you, because only we can make that choice. Our parents can't make it for us. Our friends can't make it for us. Our youth leaders, pastors, or priests, as well-meaning as they are, can't even make it for us. But the good news here is that you don't have to go it alone. Jesus promises that his Spirit will be there to guide and empower you. This is why the Scriptures say in Colossians 1:27 that Christ in you is the hope of glory. With so many examples of scandals and abuse, it can be easy to take our eyes off Jesus and join the crowd of accusers standing in judgment over the Amandas, regardless of whether they look the part. My advice: take responsibility yourself for preserving your purity. Look to Jesus for motivation and strength as you protect your innocence, demand respect from others for your body and soul, and treat people not as objects or possessions but as precious creations of God.

The Modesto Manifesto

If there is one person who has influenced the pattern of my ministry more than any other, it is Billy Graham. For years I studied his life and his legacy, and in many cases I have patterned PULSE after his best practices, the moral anchors that have kept him tethered to excellence instead of allowing him to be set adrift at sea.

For more than seven decades (let that sink in for a second: that's *seventy-plus years*), Billy Graham has been proclaiming the good news of Jesus to anyone with ears to hear. And he has done it without having any scandal break out. When I began PULSE, I decided to dig into Billy Graham's background, to try to learn how he had been able to enjoy seventy years of effective ministry, even as pastors and ministry leaders all around him were making atrocious decisions and going out in a flame of shame. I was reading Billy's autobiography *Just as I Am,* when I came across an account of when he and his three senior-most staffers, Cliff Barrows, George Beverly Shea, and Grady Wilson—all of whom would minister at his side for more than five decades' time—met in Modesto, California, where Billy was speaking.

The team was becoming better known across the country, and they sensed that God was going to expand their reach in days to come. This was 1948, but already Billy had seen his fair share of Protestant and Evangelical train wrecks. People who were rallying huge crowds in the name of Jesus were behaving in ways that were far from angelic behind the scenes. Scandal after scandal had come to light, giving all of them a bad name. He wanted his ministry to be different. He wanted to lift up the name of Jesus, not drag it through the mud. And so he met with his team to talk about the primary reasons other ministries had fallen, and what the Billy Graham Evangelistic Association, as it was known, could do to avoid them.

The team talked about the financial abuse they'd seen take place and decided that as they traveled around the world hosting events, they would always have local committees handle the offerings so that their team would never be in the position of walking away with the offering buckets, causing people to wonder how much money was raised, where the money was going, and who was benefiting from it in the end.

They talked about the misrepresentation of numbers, and how ministries often inflated their attendance to make things appear more successful than they were. A group would host an event and tell reporters that ten thousand people had attended, when in fact barely five hundred had shown up (I call this "evangelastic"). Billy and his colleagues decided that local hosts would count, record, and publish attendance figures, and that their staff would never be part of that drill.

The team also talked about the backbiting that went on among ministry agencies, and how awful it looked when believers couldn't get along. They decided to speak well of all people, even those with whom they disagreed.

But perhaps the weightiest decision that came out of those Modesto meetings was the one centered on the preservation of those men's purity. Here, they were determined to live above reproach. Billy in particular drew a clear line in the sand, deciding then and there that he would never be alone in the presence of a woman besides his wife, Ruth, even if it meant he'd have to contrive lots of wild and inconvenient solutions day by day to stick to his plan. I once read that Billy even refused to remain in an elevator car when it stopped on another floor in the hotel where he was staying and a woman stepped inside. As she stepped in, he stepped out and waited for another car to arrive.

When these four guys met and crafted their manifesto, they were good-looking twenty- and thirty-something dudes with a huge dream and the same raging hormones that course through all men of a certain age. To surrender their finances and business practices to Jesus is one thing, but to also put their sexuality in his hands? I have nothing but mad respect for that call. I firmly believe that Billy's singular decision to seek spotlessness at all costs is why at ninety-plus years old, the world still holds him in such high regard.

Billy Graham's example always begs a question of me: Do I want to live in such a way that in the final assessment, there will be an asterisk beside my name? Or do I want to leave a legacy that's asterisk free? Think about it: what comes to mind when you hear the name Tiger Woods? Maybe you reflexively think about his greatness on the golf course, about the fourteen majors he's won, about the footage of him as a two-year-old, driving a beauty on prime-time television. But my guess is that the first thought you have when you hear his name, the one that floats into your brain ahead of anything else, has something to do with his cheating on his wife and two small kids, getting caught having multiple affairs with a whole slew of women, and crashing his SUV outside of his Florida home after running away from his wife, who was chasing him down with a nine iron. Now, to be clear, God still deeply loves Tiger Woods, and it is only by the grace of God that yours and my sin isn't put on display for the world to see. But Tiger's life provides an example of what I mean by having an asterisk beside a person's name and legacy. The asterisk is the little star that leads you to the footnote that says, "Yeah. He was great at golf. But he messed up both publicly and privately in the eyes of those who mattered most."

As we've already discussed, all of us have sinned and fallen short of the glory of God (Romans 3:23). All of us have screwed up as human beings. But while all of us are sinners and all sin is essentially the same thing—rebellion against the will and ways of God—some sins are more consequential than others. Consequential sin tends to insert an asterisk beside your name. Billy Graham couldn't guarantee lack of sinfulness; even he is included in Romans 3:23. But he could guarantee with a certain amount of confidence that his sin wouldn't carry the sort of consequences that would define him and his message. If he stuck to the Modesto Manifesto, he would finish strong—no embarrassment, no asterisks, and no shame.

"Nothing on Dating?"

Right, right. A chapter on purity without a single syllable on the subject of dating is pretty unfair. So, let me offer up two quick thoughts.

First, if you are single and ready to mingle, why not focus your energy on *being* the one rather than finding the one?

I meet many students who spend every waking hour thinking about finding that special someone, when they could be taking time to allow God to change them from the inside out instead. In the same way that you cannot bring health to a friendship until you yourself are committed to living healthfully, you cannot enjoy an appropriate and productive dating relationship apart from the life and love of Jesus Christ—the inventor, giver, and sustainer of all that is right and good.

And second, remember that circumstances will not fix your character flaws but only amplify them.

If you have a purity issue now, invite God to deal with it. If you are looking to guys or girls for your identity, now is the time for a relationship reset back to the only One who matters. God knows what you need before you ask, so use this time to invite him to do a deep work on your heart.

When you are in a dating relationship in which both parties are pursuing Jesus first—before anyone or anything else—you stand a 100 percent better chance of thriving than when you settle for something less, something that dishonors God and disrespects yourself. I can say without hesitation that in almost every facet of love, waiting is better than rushing. Actually, I can't think of a single exception to this rule. It's better to wait to date. It's better to wait to pursue intimacy with another (besides God). It's better to wait to have sex. Song of Solomon 8:4 (NLT) says "not to awaken love until the time is right," which happens to be really good advice. Wait, wait, wait. You'll never regret slow and thoughtful. Focus on gathering up as much wisdom as you can, and trust that in God's perfect timing, love will be awakened in you.

Ready for a Reset?

For young men and women who want to start preserving their purity and devoting more of themselves to Jesus, I recommend two starting points:

1. First, limit your access to inputs that are going to off-road you from God's best.
2. Second, set up a few accountability structures so that you can stay the course over the long haul.

Limit Your Access

My wife and I have a rule in our marriage, which is that anything that is going to help keep our hearts turned toward God is a really good investment. This means that the Internet-filtering software we use that costs us eighty bucks a year is worth the sacrifice of those eight or nine movie tickets across the same time period. I struggled with staying pure online as a teen; why would I leave anything to chance? We think we can handle it. We even say to ourselves, "I can handle it."

Clearly, we've proven we can't. If we could handle the sexual temptation surrounding us, we'd have a lot fewer casualties.

So. Take inventory. When are you most prone to giving in to temptation? Maybe you can't swing a Snapchat account. Or an Instagram account. Or a laptop with unlimited Internet access. When you're washing your face and get soap in your eyes, you don't blow off the burning sensation and say, "Eh, I'll deal with it later." No, no: you stop everything to get the stinging gone. The same needs to be true with sin. Stop everything and get the pain out of your life.

Look for Accountability

Next, as we discussed in the last chapter, seek out a few people with whom you can talk freely about your purity goals. I once heard that whenever someone starts praying, they stop sinning, and I have found this to be true. Whenever you surround yourself with people who are committed to walking with Jesus and who have your best interest at heart, the conversations and heartfelt prayers you share help you string together one sin-free moment after another, until your affections shift from being centered on sin to being centered on the One who knew no sin, Jesus.

In my later years of high school, I gathered a group of guys to meet and talk about purity and our struggles to stay clean before God. I'm sure we all lied from time to time, but our effort to be accountable was born of sincere hearts. We wanted to be honest. We wanted to make wise choices. We wanted to live pure. And eight times out of ten, we got it about right. Find your group. Dive into real discussions. Craft your own manifesto, if you want. And watch your resolve advance.

If you don't have someone to meet with weekly for accountability, start here.

Let the Light Shine In

If I could add a third consideration to your list of purifying to-dos, it would be this: as you make your way toward more productive habits, don't forget to let the light of Jesus shine in. The goal of limiting your access to triggers and soliciting a little accountability isn't mere behavior modification or adding a layer of legalism or religiosity to your life. The goal is surrender. The goal is relationship. The goal, in short, is love.

Singer/songwriter Leonard Cohen, in his song "Anthem" wrote, "There is a crack in everything. . . . That's how the light gets in."[45] The cracks you feel—in your purity, in your self-concept, in your life—can be conduits for light to flood in. Come to the Light himself, Jesus, as you begin each and every day. Ask him for the strength to live this twenty-four-hour period pure. Claim his purity as your own. Give him permission to lead you each step of your day, trusting his presence to save your life.

Open your Bible. Get on your knees. And watch Jesus change everything.

9

Jesus, Reset My Habits

His name was Bart. And like you and me, his life was made up of routine. Get up. Clean up. Eat breakfast. Off to another day of life. The twist to this story is that Bart's full name is Bartimaeus, the blind beggar we learn of in Mark 10.

Every day, Bartimaeus would wake up, walk to the same spot in the city of Jericho, and beg. There were no social programs for blind people in Bart's day, which meant that he survived on whatever food or pocket change he could convince people to drop into his hat. He was an outcast, a nobody, a desperate person just going through the motions, indulging the same lifeless routine day after day. I think we've all been there. Whether you are literally an outcast or simply know the feeling, we've all felt "less than" in the monotony of life. Maybe you feel that way today.

Against this backdrop, Jesus shows up. On his way out of town after teaching and ministering in Jericho, the frenzied crowd that surrounded Jesus wherever he went ramps up even more as Jesus walks by the very street corner on which Bartimaeus had set up shop.

We can't know for sure, but I like to imagine that Bartimaeus was well aware of who Jesus was. Throughout the ages, people have gravitated to others like themselves, so it's not a stretch to assume the same was true in Bartimaeus's day. History tells us that those with varying disabilities would often live in community outside of town in an attempt to protect and care for one another. Bartimaeus likely had his tent next to others who were dealing with challenging conditions and was part of a group that would share whatever food—or stories—they'd collected that day. I can picture him there, warming his hands by a fire, a few of his buddies sitting at his side, when one of them says, "Hey, Bart, did you hear what happened to Eddie?"

Eddie lived around the corner from Bartimaeus and hadn't been able to walk in decades.

"You mean Bum Eddie?" Bart asks. "No! What happened?"

The guy goes on. "He can walk, Bart. Bum Eddie can walk! He was lying around like normal, begging for help, when this dude Jesus showed up. Some say he's a prophet. Others say he's crazy. Some think he's the Messiah . . . you can never be sure. All I know is that Bum Eddie was lying there and all the sudden he's hit with some kind of *Extreme Makeover: Jesus Edition.* Eddie is now leading the aerobics class for the camp, man, I kid you not."

Bartimaeus sits there, shaking his head. *Wow,* he thinks, *I wish I could meet this Jesus. I'm tired of being blind.*

I meet hundreds of people just like blind Bart. They've heard about Jesus and would even welcome some kind of divine encounter, but the knowledge doesn't change anything in their day-to-day life. Knowing the story isn't enough.

It's Hard to See When You're Blind

When I was ten years old, my cousin gave me an old pair of Oakley sunglasses he was done with. I'd never owned my own Oakleys, and when I slipped them on, I felt myself morph from ordinary North Dakota Nick to soon-to-be-discovered child movie star. I looked awesome. Check that: I *was* awesome.

I was given a new bike for my birthday—a black and (masculine shade of) purple Trek 820 mountain bike—and I decided I should ride around the neighborhood with my new shades and new wheels so that everyone else could bask in my awesomeness. It was May 27 (my birthday, in case you want to send a gift), and I remember it was warm outside. The reason I remember it was warm was that my fashion ensemble for this preliminary voyage also included my other favorite clothing items—my beloved leather bomber jacket, my acid-washed Girbaud jeans, and a sweet pair of Jordans. Ignoring the beads of sweat that were already forming on the back of my neck and under my arms, I took a look at myself in the full-length mirror in my parents' room and nodded in satisfaction. The guys in One Direction would have been proud.

Normally the streets in our neighborhood were alive with people doing yard work or hanging out with each other or coming and going from wherever. But not so on this day. *Where is everybody?* I thought, as I cruised around the block, extra slow, convinced people must be admiring my attire from inside their homes instead. Unfortunately, with all of my attention diverted to doing my best Tom-Cruise-in-*Top-Gun* impersonation, I failed to notice the parked car I was about to run into. I should mention here that the reason my cousin gave up his Oakleys is because the lenses were so scratched that to look through them was the equivalent of peering through one of those cheap kaleidoscopes they sell at Walmart, minus all the mind-blowing colors. I couldn't have seen that parked car if I'd been staring at it the entire time. All I saw was a mishmash of fragmented triangles and lines, which explains how moments later I was lying on the asphalt with blood trickling from my nose onto my bomber jacket and my Oakleys smashed into a dozen sad bits.

I didn't feel very cool anymore.

As I lay there on the ground, in a moment of mature clarity I thought about how dumb it was to sacrifice sight simply to look cool. It's hard to see when you're blind.

Stone-Blind to Brightness

One of Jesus' early followers, the apostle Paul, wrote a letter to a church in Corinth once and in it explained why some people in those days were having trouble surrendering their lives to Jesus. He wrote, "If our Message is obscure to anyone [he was talking about the message of grace here], it's not because we're holding back in any way. No, it's because these other people are looking or going the wrong way and refuse to give it serious attention. All they have eyes for is the fashionable god of darkness. They think [Satan, the enemy of God] can give them what they want, and that they won't have to bother believing a Truth they can't see. They're stone-blind to the dayspring brightness of the Message that shines with Christ, who gives us the best picture of God we'll ever get" (2 Corinthians 4:3–4).

Bloodying my nose in the name of looking cool may have been pretty inconsequential in the grand scheme of things, but as I look back on my life, I see dozens of other times when the choices I made or the actions I took blinded me to truth in deeply significant ways. These are the moments I allowed junk to creep into my life and then let it stay awhile and then let it make itself right at home. As the saying goes, "Sin takes you far away, keeps you longer than you want to stay, and costs more than you want to pay." No words could be truer than those. Seemingly insignificant allowances turned into not-so-great habits that turned into full-on barriers between God and me. It would take me time to recognize the barriers for what they were, which makes sense, doesn't it? I was blind. I couldn't see that I'd stopped growing. I couldn't see that I'd become cold toward God. I couldn't see that I was hurting myself. I couldn't see what I couldn't see, which brings me to one of the reasons I love the story of Bartimaeus: The guy absolutely refused to stay blind. The decisions and actions and habits and norms that were keeping him far from God—he wanted all of them gone. He was determined to see clearly and knew that Jesus was just the man to help.

Open Your Eyes! Jesus Is Passing By

Back to the story itself. Jesus is making his way out of Jericho, when Bartimaeus detects a distinct buzz in the air. People are flooding the road, trying to get a glimpse of Jesus, and in the midst of the commotion, the voice of a blind beggar pierces the air. "Son of David, Jesus!" Bartimaeus shouts out. "Mercy, have mercy on me!" (Mark 10:47). As Bartimaeus cries with everything inside him, the people around try to shut him up—"You're a bum! A drifter! Jesus doesn't have time for you," they jeer.

Sometimes I wonder how many times we allow others' perceptions or opinions to keep us away from going all-in for Jesus. *What will they think of me? What will they say?* It would be far easier to stay quiet and try to fit in.

Bartimaeus had no tolerance for this type of thinking. No, he was a man on a mission. Every day, his blindness had taken him to the same corner in the same city, begging for the same sorry handouts that never quite satisfied his need. Bartimaeus had had it with going through the motions. The guy was ready to see. And so, the text says that despite all the taunts and ridicule, he "yelled all the louder, 'Son of David! Mercy, have mercy on me!" (verse 48).

As I look at Bartimaeus, I see a picture of faith in high definition. He has never met Jesus, but he's willing to risk losing every other relationship to meet him. He can't see Jesus, but he is crying out for him all the same. He is holding on to hope for something he has never known before. "Jesus!" he says, full-voiced. "I need you more than anything else."

To the crowd's collective shock, Jesus stopped and heard that one small voice of Bartimaeus. To that point, Jesus always stops for those who cry out his name. Even as you read these words, I believe Jesus is passing by and willing to stop for you. As Bartimaeus experienced as he sat there in the dirt, Jesus hears your voice and longs to respond. Amid whoops and hollers rising from a thousand mouths, Jesus scans the crowd for that one voice he's heard, that one blind beggar who finally wants to see. And then he says to anyone within earshot, "Wait. Call that one person over to me" (see verse 49).

Can you imagine the electricity that fills the air as Jesus stops and calls Bartimaeus? In an instant, Bartimaeus is transformed from social outcast to homecoming king, as he's carried to Jesus' feet through what I picture as some kind of high-five tunnel of applause. Landing at the feet of his Savior, Bartimaeus then hears Jesus' voice. "What can I do for you?" Jesus asks Bartimaeus, to which the man answers, "Rabbi [meaning Teacher], I want to see" (verse 51).

"On your way," Jesus says to the man. "Your faith has saved and healed you" (verse 52). And in that very instant, Bartimaeus recovers his sight and follows Jesus down the road.

Still today, I can't read the story of blind Bartimaeus receiving sight without getting fired up. That image of finally being able to see—and really see—it's so compelling, isn't it? You and I both know how it feels to receive sight in some area of our lives and then with that fresh vision be able to acknowledge how blind we were. Maybe you broke up with a boyfriend or girlfriend and only then could see how destructive the relationship was. Or maybe you switched from one major to another and only then were able to see how unhappy you were in that first field of study. Or maybe you turned in your Samsung and bought an iPhone and only then saw how uncool you previously were. (Don't worry, I'm just . . . serious!)

My point is that this idea of going from blind to seeing is a theme Jesus doesn't want us to miss. When we surrender our lives to him, he starts smoothing out our crackled vision. He brings into focus what was previously blurred. And the thing is, all we have to do to see and really see is simply to call his name. "Jesus," we can say, just like that blind beggar did. "Mercy. Have mercy on me, please. I am done with being blind."

Jesus is passing by, in your life and in mine. He is listening for our voices above the bellowing roar of the crowd.

My Habits, Jesus' Healing

Sometimes I can get deeply discouraged by the brokenness that is crushing this generation. To me, one of the greatest tragedies of this life is when someone is blinded by their choices and habits and says no to the offer of sight. On a recent flight, I watched a documentary on singer Amy Winehouse, who allowed her drug and alcohol addiction to overtake her life. In her song "Rehab," she wrote, "They tried to make me go to rehab, I said, 'No, no, no.' "[46] The tune has a catchy Motown feel with amazing horns, and when you hear it, you can't help but sing along. But if you slow down and think about what you're actually singing and the eventual outcome of the amazing talent singing it, you can't help but cringe. "I'm a blind person who doesn't want to see," the song is basically saying. "I want my habits more than I want to be healed."

I've never struggled with substance abuse, but I've definitely known my share of destructive habits. For example, I'm a goer and a doer who has trouble sitting still. I took a personality test[47] one time that associates you with a different animal, depending on how you answer the questions. I think the four main categories were the beaver, the otter, the golden retriever, and the lion. The beaver was the dependable, detail-oriented engineer-type. The otter was the spontaneous social director. The golden retriever was the nurturing, nonconfrontational people-pleaser who made sure everyone was always okay. And then there was the lion, the hard-edged, competitive authoritarian who lives for making decisions and taking charge. I wasn't merely a lion, according to the test. I was the irritable, insomniac lion who ate the other three animals for lunch. Nice, right?

While I'm exaggerating a little, the lion was a fitting description of me. For my entire adult life, I have tried to slow down, tapping the brakes every once in a while. It's not that I don't see the benefits of a more measured pace; I do. I've even taken retreats from time to time, in essence forcing myself to stop and rest. Once I even did a multiple-day silent retreat, only to return home and dash off to the next thing, indulging for the millionth time the dead sprint that doesn't yield life. I will jokingly tell friends that I do not come with brakes, but behind the laughter is the very real possibility that if I don't keep my "run fast, run hard" approach under control, I'll lose any semblance of personal sanity while simultaneously running over the people I love. I've been around a lot of leaders whose legacy has been defined by their tendency to steamroll people, a legacy I definitely don't want for myself.

What is it for you? Perhaps the habit derailing and distancing you from God is something else entirely. Maybe you don't struggle with busyness and pushing, but instead with apathy, procrastination, or never being able to really amp up. Or maybe you struggle with overspending, gambling, eating too much, sleeping around, or being harsh. Going back to the apostle Paul's letter to the church in Corinth (1 Corinthians 6:12), he says that while we are free to do what we please, we should keep close watch not to let anything become master of our lives other than Jesus. Whatever it is, Jesus says, "I've got this. Healing can be yours, as soon as your heart is mine."

This is why Bartimaeus's story is so powerful for us. He reminds us that the only way to break a lifeless habit is to come to Jesus and ask for help. "Mercy! Have mercy on me, Jesus! I'm done with being blind."

It's really not at all surprising that Jesus stopped what he was doing and focused on Bartimaeus that day. He loves it when we choose to stop making poor choices and numbing our pain and running ourselves into the ground. He loves it when we decide that finally we're ready to see.

Habits That Truly Fulfill

Recent studies have shown the average person takes in more than five thousand advertising images each day, all of which claim to be the answer to our question about where happiness is really found.[48] The truth is that there are hundreds of habits that vie for our attention but never in a million years satisfy. Bartimaeus could have sat on that spot on that busy street, begging for decades to come, and yet he'd probably never do more than scrape by. His daily habit would never bring him real life. Amy Winehouse could have used twice as much as she did each day, but she'd never have found real peace. I can keep running and gunning and chasing to-dos, but my busyness will never equal godliness. Bartimaeus's habit was leading him to hopelessness, Amy Winehouse's habit was leading her to uncontrollable addiction, and my habit, if I'm not careful, will lead me to ice out those I say I care about and chase the elusive "all I need is a little more" dream.

Following our habits through to their logical consequences like this is a good way to gauge how well they are serving you. For example, if your habit eventually will lead to hopelessness, lifelessness, sadness, darkness, and being a jerk to family and friends, then even though that habit may seem innocent and benign today, you can be sure that on some given tomorrow, it will bite you in the . . . donkey. (Shout-out to *Shrek.*) Galatians 5:19–21 has some strong things to say about shortsighted, self-serving habits. "It is obvious what kind of life develops out of trying to get your own way all the time," those verses read. "Repetitive, loveless, cheap sex; a stinking accumulation of mental and emotional garbage; frenzied and joyless grabs for happiness; trinket gods; magic-show religion; paranoid loneliness; cutthroat competition; all-consuming-yet-never-satisfied wants; a brutal temper; an impotence to love or be loved; divided homes and divided lives; small-minded and lopsided pursuits; the vicious habit of depersonalizing everyone into a rival; uncontrolled and uncontrollable addictions; ugly parodies of community." The apostle Paul ends his rant with this: "I could go on" (verse 21). And given the sin streaks Paul knew in his own life along the way (there's a reason he called himself chief among sinners[49]), I guarantee he could.

But equally true, if your habit eventually will lead to life and love and joy and inner peace, then even though it may not feel totally exhilarating from time to time, you can be sure it is birthing something beautiful in you along the way. Simply said, when you invest in good things, you will get good results. Recent studies have shown this to be true, especially when it comes to reading the Bible. Specifically, those who read Scripture at least four times a week are less likely to engage in behaviors such as gambling, pornography, getting drunk, and sex outside marriage.[50] "My counsel is this," the apostle Paul says in Galatians 5:16–18. "Live freely, animated and motivated by God's Spirit. Then you won't feed the compulsions of selfishness. For there is a root of sinful self-interest in us that is at odds with a free spirit, just as the free spirit is incompatible with selfishness. These two ways of life are antithetical, so that you cannot live at times one way and at times another way according to how you feel on any given day. Why don't you choose to be led by the Spirit and so escape the erratic compulsions of a law-dominated existence?"

Sow good seeds, and reap a good harvest. It happens every time.

Count Your Blessings

Whenever I feel overwhelmed by the chaos before me, I try to write a to-do list. Starting a few years ago, I began every to-do list with this task: "Find the meaning of life." For those of us who know Jesus and love Jesus and live to make Jesus known, we've landed on the meaning of life. And somehow, reminding myself of that fact on days when the rest of my life feels out of control puts everything else in perspective. It reminds me that no matter what else happens today, I'm loved, I've succeeded, and because of Jesus, ultimate victory is mine. I can live my life from a place of having already won rather than pushing to win the day. Jesus reminds me that a door was opened for me that I didn't deserve to have opened, that because of the cross—his death, his sacrifice, his blood—that door of salvation swung wide open for anyone and everyone who wished to walk through. I'm reminded that in Jesus, my burden is light, even on days when heavy is all I can see. Most times, I can't even conceive of a burden that is light, but as I sit there in God's presence at the start of a day, thanking him for his goodness, reminding myself of what is true, I sense the weight being lifted. I feel the lightness arrive.

If what I'm saying is true (and it is!), then people of faith should shine the brightest, even on the darkest nights. When the money runs out or the relationship fails or the test results have bad news to report, still we can come before Jesus with words of gratitude on our lips. "Thank you for saving me. Thank you for having huge plans for my life. Thank you for seeing me, and for promising to rescue me from this pain." When everyone else panics, those who know Jesus stand out because our hope is not placed in our current position but in a person—in Jesus Christ. On the flip side, if I tell you that I trust in Jesus and yet I collapse into the fetal position every time tough circumstances show up, then while it may be true that I like Jesus or know a lot about Jesus or think that Jesus is the bomb, I'm not, in fact, trusting him. Trusting him equals contentment. Trusting him equals confidence. Trusting him equals inner peace. Trusting him equals a burden that is unbelievably and undeniably light, because the burden is simply surrendering all to him. Jesus is seated at the right hand of God at this very moment, and I can guarantee that he is not intimidated by the situations we face. When we look to him, everything else takes on a fresh perspective.

Keep Good Company

For all the reasons we discussed in the chapter on relationships, adopting and maintaining good habits is much easier when you have people in your life who love Jesus, who love you, and who are willing to help you grow in your spiritual disciplines and in your faith.

Recently, I was heading out for a tour—PULSE's biggest one to date—and for whatever reason, I was down. A friend of mine happened to call, and after I confided in him the emotional struggle I was having, he said, "Hey, Nick. I love you, bro, but let's revisit reality for a sec. You have a beautiful, supportive wife. You have a healthy, fantastic son. You have a baby girl on the way. You have a ministry that is doing well. You're off to speak on the biggest tour your organization has ever known. On every side, God is blessing you, providing for you, and giving you every resource you need to thrive. So why are you down?" He stopped and prayed for me, and in that moment, it was as if everything was okay again.

We need people in our lives who are wise. Consider permission officially granted to distance yourself from the fools. Like Mr. T says, you can "pity the fool"; just don't make them your bestie. You can always come back to minister to them, after you've steadied your own spiritual ship. But for now, the best thing for you (and them) is that you get your life in order with some wise counsel.

Put Others Above Yourself

If we spend time with Jesus, then we will naturally be driven to do the things that Jesus did. In other words, if you tell me you're hanging out with Jesus every day and yet there is no desire in your life to share your faith, or love those he gave his life for, then we should probably dig a little deeper to find out what version of Jesus we are talking about.

Jesus gave his life for others, and one of the most freeing realizations you can come to is that life isn't all about you. It's not about me, either. Life is about knowing Jesus and making him known in our service to others. Life is about extending amazing grace to people, one wretch at a time. We all start wretched; we all need to be shown the way back to God. It takes discipline to keep another's relationship with God at the forefront of your thinking, but it's a discipline you will never regret.

Start here: the next time a friend pops into your head, instead of thinking the same old thoughts about them—thoughts based on popularity, clothes, work, school, money, their family, their house, their car, and how you compare to them—try thinking about where they are with God first. How would you like others to be praying for you? I need people to pray for me, and I can guarantee the same is true of each person God has brought into your life. With that friend in mind, say, "God, please bless him today. Please be near to him in a way he can sense. Help him overcome whatever obstacles he's facing. Give me opportunities to share your hope with him."

Then, text that person and say, "Hey, thinking about you. Hope you're doing well. Praying for you today."

I try to send texts just like that every day, and I'm always amazed by the responses I get back. Not everyone responds, but when they do, they tell me what a huge deal it was for them. Think about it, when was the last text like that you got? Let's start a new trend!

Another habit I try to maintain as I'm on the go is to ask God to bring me opportunities to encourage strangers. Recently I prayed with a guy at a park. On the last tour I was speaking on, I met a worker in the stands where our event was taking place. I think he was cleaning the aisles or fixing one of the chairs. When I approached him, I said, "Hey, I'm part of the group that's putting on tonight's event, and I wanted to come say hi and to thank you for all your work to make this place look so nice." I could tell he was shocked that someone would take the time to talk to him.

That man and I wound up talking for nearly half an hour. He had some troubling stuff going on in his life, and I was able to listen, pray for him, and offer a copy of the gospel of John that we have at our events. It was such a simple thing, stopping by and saying hello. But the net effect was incredible—both for his heart and for mine. This is how it is with kindness: the rewards are always great.[51]

Stay Close to Jesus

If I had to pinpoint the most important habit of all, it's this one: get as close to Jesus as you can, as often as you can. There is no substitute for time with Jesus. In my own life and in the lives of thousands of young people across the globe, I've noticed that the deadliest habits aren't the typical suspects, such as drugs, gambling, liquor, or sex—despite how crippling those things can be. No, the deadliest habit is a little thing called distraction—the slow drift away from God. It's the subtle meandering away from the trail until the day dawns when you wake up and realize you have no idea where you are, how you got there, or how on earth you're going to find your way home.

We all drift from time to time, and while we can't ensure 100 percent close proximity to Jesus every second of every day, we can get better at spotting the drift, at training our hearts to seek him first (Matthew 6:33, NIV), and at quickly making our way back to his side. "Keep your eyes on Jesus," Hebrews 12:2 says, "who both began and finished this race we're in."

When I see that I've drifted into my work and pride, I can put my eyes back on Jesus and be reminded that it's his work I'm doing.

When I see that I've drifted into comparison and jealousy, I can put my eyes back on Jesus and be reminded that in him my life is complete, lacking nothing. In him, I have all that I need.

When I see that I've drifted into a state of depression, I can put my eyes back on Jesus and be reminded that the more I invite him into my thoughts, the more joy I will know in my soul.

And the same is true for you. Whenever you see that you've drifted from God, that there is distance between you, you can put your eyes back on Jesus and know that he's eager to welcome you back.

Practically, there are a few things I do to fix my eyes on Jesus, as the Scripture says (see Hebrews 12:2, NIV). For example, when I wake up in the morning, instead of reflexively reaching for my phone to check my social-media feeds, the first thing I do is pray through my day. I do it right there in bed, even before my feet have hit the floor. I think about where I'll be going, what I'll be doing, and who I'll be doing it with, and I offer up those people and plans to God. I ask him to redirect me whenever and however he needs so that I can live the day for him. I ask him to give me wise words to say. I ask for the grace to be kind to people instead of ignoring them, dismissing them, or manipulating them. I ask for him to keep me far from bad decisions, decisions that in an instant could wreck my life. And I thank him for promising to accompany and equip me as I go about my day.

Once I get going, I try to read a passage of Scripture, either with the YouVersion app on my phone or else in the Bible that sits on my nightstand. Sometimes I read a devotional book, such as Sarah Young's *Jesus Calling* or the old classic *Streams in the Desert.* Today's entry says, "It is very easy to fall into the habit of doubting, worrying, wondering if God has forsaken us, and thinking that after all we have been through, our hopes are going to end in failure. But let us refuse to be discouraged and unhappy! Let us 'consider it pure joy' (James 1:2, NIV), even when we do not feel any happiness."[52] Something as simple as that truth can ground my entire day. As long as it's grounded in Scripture, I find it to be an anchor. I bet the same would be true for you.

If I'm in my car for an extended period of time, I'll listen to worship music. If I need to blow off some steam and go for a run, I'll queue up a sermon from a beloved pastor and grow spiritually while I log my miles. If I get bad news that sends me reeling emotionally, I'll mutter under my breath, "Jesus, Jesus, Jesus. Help me, Jesus." People nearby might think I'm cursing, but I'm not. I'm trying to keep from falling apart. I'm trying to stay connected to him, because things tend to devolve quickly whenever I flee his scene.

And that's my point here: do whatever you need to do to get Jesus, because there is no substitute for time spent with him.

Residual Blessings

I once heard someone say that it's impossible to walk toward God and walk away from him at the same time. And while that might seem obvious, it's a helpful picture to keep in mind. The reason the good habits we've talked about—being thankful, surrounding yourself with wise people, being kind, and staying close to Jesus—are good is because they spur us on toward God instead of seducing us to walk away. But there's more. Because another useful fact to keep in mind regarding good habits is that they benefit your life not just in the moment, but for years and years to come. I call this dynamic the "residual blessing," and it's a really cool thing to behold.

When Tiffany was first pregnant a few years ago with our son, Truett, it seemed like it took forever before she and I could tell she was actually pregnant. She looked the same. She seemed the same. Her same jeans still fit. For months and months this was true, until one day, *poof!* Her belly started expanding, and we finally had visible proof that our son was in there growing. Prior to that, she and I would get these updates once or twice a week from a website for expecting couples that tracked the size and development of your baby, based on when the woman became pregnant. During those early weeks, we'd read that our baby was the size of a poppy seed, and then a lima bean, and then a green olive, and then a pea pod, and then a lemon. On and on the descriptions went, always reflecting an increase in size, and for reasons we never could figure out, always pertaining to food.

The website would swear that all this activity was unfolding inside my wife, even as nothing obvious had changed on the outside. She'd lament this fact from time to time, saying she was totally exhausted from being pregnant, even though there wasn't yet anything to show from all her hard work. I'd say, "Honey, you are doing great! Who cares what else you get done this afternoon? You made *eyelids* for our *child* today. You rock!"

I think this is how it goes sometimes with spiritual disciplines, the good habits that we choose to practice even when we don't see any demonstrative results. Once you get into the habit of being grateful, for instance, someday you'll face a really challenging situation, and instead of crumbling, you'll whisper a prayer of thanksgiving. "God, thanks for being with me in this. Thanks for helping me prevail."

If you get into the habit of being caring and accepting, the day will come when you'll find yourself having a meaningful conversation about Jesus with someone you would have judged or criticized before. God will start giving you amazing opportunities to talk about him with people who need him, because you are living for him.

If you get into the habit of surrounding yourself with wise people, you'll start noticing how much easier it is to draw healthy boundary lines in your relationships, to say no to invitations to sin, to invest time and energy in life-giving community like a local church or a small group or a campus Bible study. That wisdom you're around starts seeping into your mind and heart, and over time, you too become wise.

If you study in school, your grades get better. If you run a mile every day, your endurance gets stronger. And if you practice good habits, your love for God grows. I think this is why he went to the trouble of laying out in his Word the practical habits we should be practicing, because he knows that when we commit ourselves to those habits, our affections get ordered in a way that honors him, a concept we'll explore further in chapter 10.

"We program our priorities," a friend of mine once told me. "If something is important to you, then it will show up in your daily routine." If sleep is the most important thing in my life, then I will log ten or twelve hours in bed. If partying is the most important thing in my life, then I'll orient my world around that scene. If sex is the most important thing in my life, then I'll pour all my energy into the chase. But if Jesus is in that top spot, then I'll devote myself to knowing him, loving him, serving him, and telling the people in my life how they can do the same.

When Jesus is our chief habit, our attitude improves. Our wisdom increases. Our perspective expands. Our confidence surges. Our faith upturns. When Jesus is our habit, all of life advances, because it is Jesus who changes everything, and the changes he enacts are always good.

Ready for a Reset?

Despite the thousands of good habits we could talk about, according to the broad-brush themes of the Bible, I'd like to offer two basic categories: "sit and wait" habits and "go and do" habits. God says we are to be still and know that he is God, and that we are to wait on his voice and his guidance and his peace. And then he says that faith without works is dead faith, and that a primary purpose in our lives is to go and share the gospel with people who need to be saved.

Jesus says, "Come into my presence. Still your mind. Quiet your thoughts.

Hear from me. And then take the grace and peace I've given you to a chaotic and embittered world."

If you crave a reset in your daily routine, then this two-part sequence is for you. First, sit and wait. And then, in God's name, go and do.

Sit and Wait

Tomorrow, start your day with a simple prayer. Before your feet hit the floor, say, "God, today I want to follow you. I want to hear your voice. I want to feel joy and peace and fulfillment. I want to live today as your child." After you pray, open up a passage of the Bible and read until a verse strikes you as relevant to the situation you're in. Write the verse down—log it in your phone, grab a dry-erase pen and jot it down on your mirror, scribble it on your hand (the original PalmPilot)—and come back to it throughout your day, letting the power of God's truth wash over you again and again.

Go and Do

Next, as you work to stay in conversation with God throughout your day, ask him to give you the strength and courage to practice being grateful and kind and wise. Start with little things, like making eye contact with a stranger and saying hello, or reaching out to a friend with an encouraging word, or changing the subject when a friend starts gossiping to you about someone, or saying thanks but no thanks when you're offered the drink or the pill or the bong or whatever the thing is that usually leaves you deflated and derailed.

Day by day, add a few small habits that lead to life, and subtract a few that don't. Over time, you'll be remade. As Paul said in another of his famous letters—this one to the church in Rome—"Do not conform to the pattern of this world, but be transformed by the renewing of your mind. Then you will be able to test and approve what God's will is—his good, pleasing and perfect will" (Romans 12:2, NIV). That renewal is waiting for you.

10

Jesus, Reset My Affections

Based on my obsessive childhood endeavors, I was evidently born an entrepreneur. I was the kid who was always looking for a deal that promised to deliver whatever the consumer culture around me was pitching. Whether it was baseball cards, dirt bikes, sports cars, or basketball shoes, if there was a hook for the top-shelf item, from the earliest age I could be hooked. There's something about reaching for that shiny object that is just beyond your grip, isn't there? (Although, if my memory serves me well, climbing for a top-shelf item at the grocery store once landed me in the ER, after that candy rack came tumbling down on my head.)

I tended to justify my insatiable desire for the latest thing by explaining that I had a crazy-strong work ethic and was willing to save for all those toys. I mowed lawns, for instance. I did odd jobs around my neighborhood. I had a monopoly on the lemonade-stand market. And once, I even built modest wooden hearts and sold them from the curb. (Little did I know that what I thought was a big day of sales was in fact a pity parade of my relatives' friends, who all had been pointed toward my street to support my cause.)

At nine years old, I was captivated with two things in particular: sports cars and basketball legend Michael Jordan (I already told you about my letter to him). While I obviously was too young to get a car, that didn't stop me from keeping a notebook with me at all times, where I'd log the cars I saw. I had a top-twenty list of favorites, ranging from the diminutive Mazda Miata to the Ferrari Testarossa. I'll let you guess which of those two I caught sight of more often in Fargo. Oh, to live in New York or LA.

On the Michael Jordan side, Air Jordan shoes and clothing were a little more within reach. The first edition Jordans were released by Nike during Michael Jordan's rookie season—1984, the year he was drafted by the Chicago Bulls—and legend has it that because the shoes didn't conform to the NBA's uniform policy (they were the wrong colors), Nike had to cough up five grand in fees every single time Jordan took the court. Given the league's eighty-two-game season, it was a pretty expensive fashion choice. Except that now everyone wanted those shoes and was willing to pay a lot of money to get them. In fact, the first fourteen editions remain in such high demand that Nike started releasing retro versions of them and retailing them at super-steep prices. Now, more than ten years after Michael Jordan retired from professional basketball, Jordans are still the number one sports sneaker in the world, outpacing the second most popular shoe (LeBron James's brand) by nearly double. I think it's safe to say those five-thousand-dollar penalty payments ended up being a good investment.

In elementary and middle school, every penny I earned I saved toward the purchase of new toys. And my favorite toy to buy was a new pair of Jordans. Once I bought them, I did my best to keep them looking nice. They were precious to me, the pearl of great price, the earthly possession I would have rushed into the burning house to save. During that season of life, things were tight for my family financially. My dad was between jobs, and we were forced to move out of our home and into an apartment to cut costs. Suffice it to say, keeping up with my friends' tradition of purchasing the latest and greatest every year wasn't exactly in the plan, making my purchases all the more valuable.

Fast-forward to a few years ago, when I was in Portland for a speaking event. I reached out to some friends, in hopes of visiting Nike's headquarters. After a few calls, I connected with a guy who works at Nike who gave me the total hookup. Not only did he set up a tour for me, but he also got me a pass to visit the Nike employee store. Once inside the store, I took in the floor-to-ceiling Jordan display and was taken right back to those memories of being a little kid and wanting nothing more in the world than a new pair of shoes. I bought a Jordan duffle that day and proceeded to fill it with Christmas gifts for family, and a brand-new pair of Jordans for yours truly. They were white, and I was happy. It was a really, really good day.

After Portland, I started wearing my Jordans on occasion, and every time I did, people commented on them. I enjoy cool shoes as much as the next guy, but I never received as many compliments on my footwear as I did whenever I wore those shoes. It was uncanny. People would ask about them, and I'd tell them about the Nike employee store experience, and about the memories it had conjured up of when I was a pint-size MJ fanatic. Which would lead to fun conversations about shoes or about basketball or about Jordan himself, and before I knew it, I'd be spouting off random facts about my childhood idol—that he was born on February 17, 1963, in Brooklyn, New York, that he moved to Wilmington, North Carolina, as a kid, and that he attended Laney High School, where he didn't make the varsity team until his junior year. We would talk about his game-winning shot as a Tar Heel and about how, beginning in 1990, the Jordan-led Bulls never lost three games in a row, and about where I was during the 1992 NBA Finals when Jordan dropped six three-pointers and thirty-five points in the first half, and about the 1997 "flu game" when MJ defied all odds against the Utah Jazz.

Wearing Jordan shoes weren't only about footwear; they were time capsules to my being "like Mike," accessories for looking cool, getting respect, and talking basketball all day long. If I had the resources, I probably would have bought ten more pairs. Thankfully, I didn't. More on that in a moment.

Just Don't Mess with My Stuff

Jesus told a story one time about a young man who had the finances to fund as many Ferraris or pairs of Jordans as he wished. This guy had it all: money, good looks, a winning smile, and the relational and emotional deference reserved for people who are rich, handsome, charming, and strong. This guy went down in history as the "rich young ruler," which pretty well sums up what we are all after, doesn't it? Who wouldn't want to be young, affluent, attractive, and in charge?

One day, our young friend (let's call him Rich) comes up to Jesus and says, "Listen, I've done everything you said I have to do, to get my ticket to heaven. I don't kill people. I don't commit adultery. I don't steal, and I don't lie. I'm cool with my mom and dad, and I try to love my neighbor as myself—including even people who like cats. What else do I have to do to get into heaven? What more has to happen before I can get this thing called 'eternal life'?"[53]

Jesus thinks for a minute and then says, "Listen, if you are serious about this, if you really want to go all-in with God, then here's what you need to do: go sell all your possessions—your house, your sweet ride, your phone, your clothes, and yes, even your beloved Jordans. Sell all that stuff. Give to the poor. Then come follow me."

I want you to imagine this scenario for a moment. Chances are that you aren't known by your friends as a rich young ruler. But no matter your financial standing, this is a pretty intense invitation, right? Get rid of everything? Even my iPhone, Jesus? My car? Why do you need my Jordan 3s?

Billy Graham calls this invitation of Jesus' the "high cost of low living," and Rich knew right away he couldn't do what Jesus asked. He was dejected as he walked away, thinking about how impossible it would be to part with his things: *Don't you know that you can only be Lord of my life, Jesus, if you agree not to mess with my stuff?*

When I was graduating from high school, I convinced my parents that I needed a new car. "Convinced" would be a gracious way to describe what I did; manipulated is more the case. After months of pestering them for this car, I ended up needing a kidney surgery that had my loving parents on their knees, in desperate prayer for their son's very life. So, right before I went in for the operation, while Mom and Dad were hanging on to my every word, I looked longingly into their eyes and said, "Mom . . . Dad. I love you." (It was Oscar-worthy, really.) "There's just one thing I want to ask you before I go under for this operation." Leaning in for these final words, I went for the jugular. "Can I please have the car?"

My parents caved, and I was victorious. Or so I thought, anyway.

Not surprisingly, that new car was never quite as satisfying as I thought it would be. While I loved being the object of envy as I pulled onto campus, it didn't take long before there was a nicer car I wanted more. Not to mention, the manipulation I employed in order to acquire the car didn't help my conscience one bit.

During the same season I was fasting to try to hear God's voice regarding my decision to play basketball, it seemed like the issue of my car kept coming up. Jesus didn't just want my hoops habit, as it turned out; he also wanted my heart. This meant that anything that had become an idol in my life would have to go. I'd only had that car for one year when I decided to go to my parents, apologize for my deception, and downgrade to an older model that wouldn't consume my affections.

Yes, Jesus is familiar with the rich-young-ruler syndrome. It's the attitude that says, "What's the big deal about eternal treasures? Look at this bling I'm rocking right now!" When Rich was out of earshot, Jesus turned to his buddies who were standing there and said, "Do you have any idea how difficult it will be for Rich to enter God's kingdom? Let me tell you, it's easier to gallop a camel through a needle's eye than for a guy like that to get in."

The Rest of the Story

It's easy to relate to Rich. I think we all know the feeling of wanting to follow Jesus without letting go of something we love just a little bit more. We look at his life of possessions, wealth, and power and think, *Is there anything so wrong with that?* We read about his good behavior, the rules he kept, the dos and don'ts he obeyed, the stars dotting his chore chart, and something in us says, "Doesn't he deserve it? Didn't he earn it? Isn't it okay to have some fun and enjoy life?" We think about how easy it would have been for Jesus to let the guy off a little easier: "Even 25 percent would be a great donation, Jesus. He clearly wants to know you; can't you cut him some kind of a break?"

And yet Jesus' instructions are there in plain language for all to read: "Sell everything you own. Give to the poor. And then come, follow me."

Is this what's required of us too? Sometimes I fear we are a generation of rich young rulers, people who want Jesus as long as it doesn't cost us any of our stuff.

The story of the rich young ruler messes with us, because we read Jesus' words and think that they must mean we too have to ditch everything we know and love in this life in order to follow him. We read Jesus' words and draw the conclusion that destitution must be a prerequisite to salvation, in the same way that you stand a chance of getting an A in calculus only if you've first passed algebra and geometry. We read Jesus' words and see a cosmic killjoy behind them, a petty tyrant who has something against nice cars and cool shoes.

And yet that's not at all what Jesus was saying when he told Rich to go sell his stuff. Or at least, it wasn't all he was saying. It pays to read the rest of the tale.

Picking up where we left off, Rich has just walked away, Jesus has just told his friends that it was going to take some serious spiritual gymnastics for someone like Rich to gain eternal life, and now those friends are standing there shocked. They look at Jesus with incredulity etched on their faces and blurt out, "Then who has any chance at all!"

It wasn't a question as much as a demand: "Come on, Jesus! Cut us some slack!"

But Jesus stayed his course. "No chance at all if you think you can pull it off yourself," he said. "Every chance in the world if you trust God to do it" (Matthew 19:26).

Peter, Jesus' friend who could often be found with his foot in his mouth, said, "We left everything and followed you. What do we get out of it?" (Can you imagine saying this to Jesus?)

In response, Jesus dropped a bomb. The rest of the rich young ruler's story is this: to everyone who follows Jesus with a full heart, on that day when Jesus takes complete control over the universe—the new heaven and the new earth—those people who have sacrificed home and family and material possessions and every other temporarily awesome thing will get it all back a hundred times over. We will recoup everything we gave up, to the tune of one hundred times our initial investment. And on top of that return, we will net eternal life. We will have our minds blown with excessive blessing, and we will live forever at Jesus' side. The last verse of Matthew 19 calls this the "Great Reversal: many of the first ending up last, and the last first" (verse 30).

"All the things you've done," Jesus was essentially saying, "all the places you've been, all the people you know, all the mountains of shiny stuff—none of it can satisfy you like I can. Loosen your grip on your stuff so that you can tighten your grip on me. I will give you life. I will give you joy. I will bless you in ways you could never secure for yourself. Yes, this plan will cost you everything. But you'll get everything and more in return."

The Great Reversal in Everyday Life

The back story on that kidney operation I mentioned earlier is that for the latter part of my senior year of high school, I experienced excruciating back pain. The summer afterward, I was scheduled to go to Uganda with a team that my youth pastor was leading, and even though I was stoked about going and had worked my tail off to raise all the funds, I was told by a very somber doctor that one of my kidneys was bad. This was a problem, he said, because unless I took care of this medical issue immediately, that kidney could rupture, and I could fall into a coma and/or die.

While I didn't know much about kidneys, I was certain I didn't want to fall into a coma and/or die. Which meant there would be no Uganda trip.

This news was especially distressing because it came on the heels of a really pathetic finish to my short-lived basketball career. The spring hadn't unfolded the way I had hoped, and despite my wild devotion to being the first player at practice, and running faster and harder and longer than anyone else on the team, and staying until I was the last guy in the gym, my visions of future sports stardom were slipping as fast as was my health. I was . . . irritated, to put it mildly. I wanted my health back. I wanted my trip to Africa back. I wanted my plans back, my dreams back, my life back. And for a few minutes, anyway, I wanted those things more than God.

Fortunately, those rebellious minutes passed quickly, and I was reminded that I could trust God. Some Bible verses came to mind, and it was as if Jesus was saying to me, "Nick, when you're weak, I'll make you strong. When you're last, I'll make you first. When you're sick, I'll make you well. When you live low, I'll lift you up." I could see then that Jesus wasn't sitting up in heaven, scanning the earth for joy to kill. No, he was eyeing every corner of the earth to find the one heart who was faithful to him (see 2 Chronicles 16:9). I wanted to be that faithful one. I wanted his gaze to land on me.

To do that, I'd have to choose to put my love for Jesus ahead of my desire for perfect health, which is exactly what I did that day. And while I was still blind to my enormously selfish pursuit of a car, I prayed to God that I'd adopt the posture Matthew talks about in his gospel, that of not being "so preoccupied with *getting,* so you can respond to God's *giving*" (6:31). Sometimes God gives us exactly what we want to show us he is better. Other times God takes away what we think will satisfy only to show where real treasure is found.

The whole world was mine for the taking—health and wholeness included—as long as I didn't put that whole world before God. And the same is true for you. Which is why we have to ask ourselves, is our love of rap or movies or friends or money or SportsCenter or whatever simply an enjoyable interest for us, or has it veered toward becoming an idol? Is it an interest or an idol? That's the real question here.

A few years after my kidney travails (which God miraculously healed that same summer, by the way), my friends and I started PULSE, and while most everyone in my relational circle was thrilled, my mom and a few others close to me were less than ecstatic. While others disapproved because of the financial uncertainty associated with full-time ministry, my mom's lack of enthusiasm had little to do with lack of support and rather with her being one of the few who understood the spiritual and emotional cost of taking on such a task. My mom is a prayer warrior and always wanted us kids to count the cost. While she loved the idea of PULSE, like most parents, she wasn't sure she wanted me traipsing across the globe, traveling in unfamiliar places, speaking in hostile settings, and calling people to respond to the most divisive message the world's ever known. Plus, this calling (along with other invitations for me to travel overseas) was happening in fall of 2001, right after the Twin Towers had fallen on 9/11. I'm pretty sure Mom thought the Taliban was going to be wherever it was I was going, and that I would never make it out of whichever country I was in alive, with limbs still attached. "Are you sure this is God's voice you are hearing?" she'd ask with pleading eyes, as though maybe I'd misinterpreted things and was just suffering from indigestion instead.

As I listened to opinions coming from every direction regarding what I should do with my life, I often felt like a ship that had entered the Bermuda Triangle. What was my North Star going to be? Whose voice would I listen to above all others—that of well-intentioned friends and family members, or that of God alone?

A few years into PULSE's existence, I found myself flying from one city to the next to speak for youth events with the Billy Graham team. I was weary from the incessant travel, and as I looked for my seat, I asked the flight attendant if there were any empty rows I could catch a nap in. She told me to go ahead and find my seat, and that she would come find me if something was available.

I sat down, and moments later a young man in army fatigues sat down next to me. He was eighteen, maybe nineteen, years old, fresh out of basic training. Exhausted, I reluctantly struck up a conversation with him, only to learn that he was equally tired. His name was Cody, he said, and his stress level was way high these days because he was being deployed to the Middle East. Our conversation went deep quickly, and as I was digging in to really understand his story, the flight attendant approached and said there was an open row that would provide my new friend and me some much-needed space for rest. We shook hands, and I stood up, headed toward the open seat a few rows up.

I'd just settled into my new spot, when a voice in my head said, *Go back and tell Cody about me.*

Ugh. It was God.

I'm supposed to go back to the seat I just left and interrupt Cody's rest to talk about Jesus? I said to God, to which he said, *Go back and pray for him.*

I tried reasoning with God. *I am going to look like a nut job going back there!* I said. *You clearly don't get frequent-flyer etiquette. I can't go back.*

God was silent in reply, which to me meant that maybe I'd won our little battle. But then, interestingly, I discovered that as I tried to enjoy my newfound peace and space in my seat, I couldn't get comfortable at all.

Okay, God, I whispered in my spirit. *If you want me to do this, then you need to make sure I don't make a complete idiot of myself. And I need you to multiply my sleep later on.* (Why I thought negotiating with God was a good idea, I'll never know.)

I stood up, and as I approached the row where Cody sat, he gave me a bewildered look. It was a look that said, "I thought you wanted some space, a chance to spread out and sleep." And that had been what I wanted. But the truth was, I wanted Jesus more. Ninety minutes later, as our plane's wheels touched down again, Cody and I were still sitting there, side by side, as he prayed to invite Jesus to lead his life. I'll never forget that flight.

Candidly, there are dozens of examples I could share of times I wish I had responded differently to God's voice. But I've always found that stories of success are far more motivating than those of regret. God is always looking for those who will listen to his voice above anyone else's.

In a thousand ways, every day of every week, we all fight for comfort over responding to Jesus' invitation for us to give everything. We tell Jesus that we don't have time for him this morning because we have to get to school or work or the gym. We tell him that we can't reach out to that person because our friends will think we're uncool. We tell him we can't let go of our need for comfort, or our need for sleep, or our need to be needed, or our sports-team fanaticism, or our car, or the boat, or the golf addiction, or movies, or drinking, or drugs, or overeating, or overspending, or the risk-seeking that tends to take us too close to the edge, because without that thing, whatever that thing is, we . . . just . . . might . . . die. Or worse yet, we never talk to Jesus at all, imagining that he doesn't want anything to do with such petty details of life. All the while, our actions tell him these things are true, that our treasure is found somewhere else. We gather up all our affections, conveniently leaving Jesus totally off of the list, and then we miss out on the stuff of real living, all because we're too busy trying to live large.

"I am here for you and not going anywhere," Jesus says in response. "I am better than all of it. Prioritize your relationship with me. Order your affections around who I am, and you'll find satisfaction you've never known."

Valuing Jesus More

At one of the first PULSE events we ever did, I explained to the crowd that one of the worst things a person can do is to invite Jesus into his or her life but then never let him fully make himself at home. It's like we open the door of the house of our heart and say to Jesus, "Sure. Come on in." But then we stand there awkwardly in the entryway like he's a door-to-door salesman who has interrupted our dinner to try to sell us carpet care. We're guarded. Put out. More than a little annoyed. And so Jesus, being the gentleman he is, recedes into the shadows, waiting for a better welcome than that.

In Jesus' day, he had strong words for people who said they were believers but who kept intimacy with him at bay. He called them "whitewashed tombs" (Matthew 23:27, NIV), people who looked sparkly and clean on the outside but who were dead men walking in their hearts. Jesus wanted nothing to do with religious show. He wanted people who were really willing to turn to him. "Change your life, not just your clothes," God said through his prophet Joel.

"Come back to God, *your* God. And here's why: God is kind and merciful. He takes a deep breath, puts up with a lot, this most patient God, extravagant in love, always ready to cancel catastrophe. Who knows? Maybe he'll do it now, maybe he'll turn around and show pity. Maybe, when all's said and done, there'll be blessings full and robust for your God!" (Joel 2:13–14).

Another translation says it this way: "rend your hearts and not your garments" (Joel 2:13, ESV), which means, don't just paste on the designation of "Christian." Instead, fully devote yourself to Christ.

Hillsong United does a song by William Murphy that I love. It says, "Give me one pure and holy passion. Give me one magnificent obsession . . ."[54] This has become my prayer of late, that I would have a singular magnificent obsession, and that that thing would be Jesus himself. Not family. Not friends. Not church. Not church people. Not Jordans. Not PULSE. Not an event—no matter how big it might be. Not all the entryways of my life. I want that obsession to be him, my risen, rescuing Lord. More than the tilt of my heart toward my wife, my kids (yes, it's now plural; Truett's adorable sister, Ruby, was born just last night), my friends, my job, my bank account, my health, my wardrobe, my political candidates, my sports teams, my dreams, my goals, my plans, my cravings, and my desires, I want my heart to feel tilted toward Jesus alone. I want my primary treasure to be a spiritual one—namely, an obsession with the person of Jesus.

In Psalm 27:4 (NIV), David said the one thing that he sought was this: to "dwell in the house of the Lord all the days of my life." The apostle Paul said that he had learned to be content in all circumstances, thanks to the abiding presence of God. And if I could be known for one thing upon my death, it would be that I'd fully trusted Jesus with my life, that on my affections list, he took the top spot. Whatever I'm known for, I want people to know that I lived my life for Jesus. You'll never regret wanting the same.

Ready for a Reset?

The reason I wanted to introduce the subject of habits before this chapter on affections is because once we nail some good habits, good affections will naturally follow. The rich young ruler knew all too well what it was like to have such a tight grip on his earthly stuff that he unwittingly bypassed eternally cool things, and if you are nodding your head in recognition of that dynamic, then let me give you two grip-loosening ideas. First, test God in his promise to return your sacrifice a hundredfold. And second, before you tend to your other affections, tend to your soul.

Test God

In Luke 4, Jesus tells us not to put God to the test by questioning his presence. However, there is one place where God tells us we *can* test him, and it's in this area of his returning to us whatever we've sacrificed in abundance—one hundredfold. In Malachi 3:10, he says, "Test me in this and see if I don't open up heaven itself to you and pour out blessings beyond your wildest dreams." Bottom line: you can't outgive God.

My encouragement to you is to go ahead and give up whatever is standing between you and him. Just let it go, in his powerful name. Now don't do this with some expectation that it will trigger a magic-genie mechanism. Only surrender it if you want to see God's faithfulness in your life. God is not after your favorite thing; God is trying to *be* your favorite thing. If you want to receive the blessing that is waiting for you, then put God in that top spot. Start to prioritize spending time with him, praying to him, reading his Word, memorizing his Word, loving like he loves, serving like he serves, and living like he lives. You start ordering your affections around Jesus, and I assure you, you'll live a blessed life.

Tend to Your Soul

Next, as you take baby steps toward prioritizing Jesus in your life, I want you to keep one image in your mind. Fair warning: it's a morbid one, but one that makes a strong point. Picture yourself lying on your deathbed, doctors surrounding you, sorrowfully shaking their heads. From your semicomatose state, you can hear them whispering to your loved ones, "I'm so sorry. We've done all we can do."

You sort of groan a final groan and slowly turn over onto your side, which is when you catch sight of your reflection in the window of your hospital room, and that is when you notice that what's clutched to your chest is . . .

What?

A Nike box? Car keys? A wine bottle? Drug paraphernalia? A credit card? A dumbbell? A ticket stub? Or maybe it's something nobler you're clinging to—your mom, your dad, your best friend, your coach, your youth pastor, your uncle, your dog.

The reality for you and me both is that on that day when we inhale our final breath, only one thing will fit in our grip, and that one thing is our soul's allegiance—to Jesus, or to nothing at all. "What good would it do to get everything you want and lose you, the real you?" Jesus asks in Mark 8:37. "What could you ever trade your soul for?"

Which is exactly the point I'm making: at all costs, tend to your soul.

11

Jesus, Reset My Generation

As I announced in the last chapter, my wife and I just welcomed our baby girl, Ruby, into the world. As Tiffany and I introduce her to people in our life, two things always happen. The first is that they ooh and ahh and tell us how cute and perfect Ruby is. (I happen to think they're correct.) The second is that they ask, "Why Ruby?"—as in, why did we pick that name.

I think what they're after here is some explanation of how it relates to our family history, or, even better, some story of spiritual revelation where we discovered that the name for "perfect girl" in the original Greek is "Ruby." This is probably why it's so anticlimactic when we instead respond with, "We just really liked the name." After enough disappointed gazes, I've committed myself to searching all the ancient languages until I discover some awesome answer. (Tweet me if you find one, please.)

I've seen this disappointment before. After Truett was born, in answer to the "Why Truett?" question, we'd tell people the story—we heard the name at Chick-fil-A, as their founder was named Truett Cathy, and we thought the name was awesome. While we felt weird saying our firstborn's name had more to do with fast food than inspiration from fasting, I began to hand out free chicken sandwich coupons in an attempt to soften the blow.

Perhaps it's this lack of sentimentality that explains why for quite some time, our ministry's name—PULSE—meant little more to me than the fact that it sounded cool. I'd had that vision the summer before my freshman year of college—"Christ at the pulse of a generation"—but I'd never really explored the significance of the term. And yet, as is so often the case, God would provide people in my path who would show me why the name mattered—and mattered deeply. Those people would help me see that just as our physical pulse shows we're still alive, our spiritual pulse declares that this life is eternal.

Over time, I would see connections between our physical pulse and our spiritual pulse nearly everywhere I looked. Just as a heart's in-beat draws blood into organs to clean it, and the physical out-beat oxygenates the blood so it can bring life to the body, the spiritual in-beat of unity and empowerment feeds the out-beat of life-giving purpose. Christ at the pulse . . . now it was all making sense.

I would start to see that this was God's vision for our generation, that we would rely on him—his presence, his power, his plan—every bit as much as we rely on our heartbeat's pounding throughout our day. On the surface, it seemed too far out of reach—an entire generation with Jesus at its pulse? And yet the world had seen it happen before, one example of which was in 1904.

When Jesus Spreads Like Wildfire

In 1904, in the country of Wales, things were turned totally upside down. Technically, things were turned right side up, but more on that in a minute. Several years before, churches around the world were being stirred to seek Jesus. The Methodists had a plan for evangelizing the entire United States. The Baptists and Presbyterians were going to give them a run for their money. And a whole chorus of prayers for revival were rising from every corner of Europe, Asia, and Australia. It seemed like everyone who loved Jesus thought it would be cool to have a worldwide conversion explosion on January 1, 1900, and so churches worked like crazy toward that goal.

This, incidentally, was the era influenced by D. L. Moody and Charles Spurgeon who had been on the scene preaching the gospel, so maybe the events to come were directly related to the faithfulness and fervency of their generation—who knows. What is known is what happened next.

The story began when a local church pastor in the tiny seaside town of New Quay, Wales, began calling his church to a deeper loyalty to Jesus. He proclaimed this message on Sunday mornings, during his church's typical worship service. But when dozens and dozens of people started responding to Jesus, the pastor decided to up the stakes. He started a Wednesday-night service and told people to come to that too, and before long the twice-weekly meetings were having such a transformative effect on people's lives that the men and women getting saved were then heading over to nearby towns and villages to tell other churches what was happening. Honestly, I'm not sure we would have a clue what to do if we were sitting through a church service on a typical Sunday and six people barged into the room, grabbed the microphone from the worship team and began to testify to their radical change. Awkward, anyone? (We actually experienced something like this at an event once when students who gave their lives to Jesus immediately went and tried to convert the concession workers. While a few prayed with these students, the venue management asked us to please control our attendees. Oops.)

The church crowd in Wales was rocked by what was happening. Word of God's movement spread like wildfire, and churches everywhere began adding prayer and outreach events to their own calendars and inviting everyone in their neighborhoods to come check out what Jesus was up to.

Newspaper quarterlies that generally promoted nothing more exciting than the town-wide rummage sale started running rarely-before-seen headlines about big crowds and God and the big crowds that were coming to hear about God. So many people flooded the small towns in Wales to hear the gospel that local grocery stores ran out of food and churches ran out of space. Some reports say that the ballooned attendance at those churches stuck around for more than twenty years. We're talking full-on widespread revival.

"Do It Again!"

The Welsh Revival rippled all throughout South Wales, North Wales, Scotland, England, and even California, thanks to the work of some passionate British missionaries, and in a single year catalyzed at least one hundred thousand people responding to Jesus in Wales and as many as one million responses throughout Great Britain. In areas where the impact was most intense, the crime rate fell to an all-time low, judges had no cases to try because nobody was committing crimes, taverns were forced to file for bankruptcy because so many people ditched their liquor habit, and cops were faced with unemployment, which caused them to pursue singing instead. For real. One police department in particular divided itself into trios and quartets and deployed themselves to the various church services being held to lead music. What else were they supposed to do in the face of a spotless society like theirs?

When my buddies and I were meeting each week in anticipation of PULSE's official kickoff—this would have been late 2004 through early 2005—we would read old newspaper articles or books about revivals like this one. That may sound like an odd thing to do when you're twenty years old, living on a college campus, free from parental rule. But we were captivated, I'll be honest. We had seen enough of godless living at our school to last us a lifetime, and given the rampant addictions and penetrating depression and climbing suicide rate closing in on us, we knew something somewhere had to give.

Rebelling against God wasn't working. Maybe surrendering to him would. Someone told me that "Revival is God's arrival." And we were convinced the only answer was God showing up.

At one of those prayer meetings, I played a twenty-minute sermon from a guy named J. Edwin Orr, a British scholar on revival who lived during the early twentieth century. In that talk, Orr recounted the miracles that happened during and after the Welsh Revival, and while his monotone voice couldn't have been more boring, his content was pure gold. That revival had happened exactly one hundred years prior to those days when my friends and I would sit in the coffee shop, praying our hearts out for change to occur on our campus, and the more information we learned about how Wales was taken by storm for Jesus, the more our prayers got distilled into one simple but soulful plea: "Do it again, God! Do it again."

Orr generally stuck to the facts about revivals that had occurred throughout history, but I'll never forget how he opened his talk on the Welsh Revival in particular. "It is no secret what God can do," he said. "What he's done for others, he'll do for you. What he's done before, he can do again."[55] Orr had been deceased for nearly twenty years by that time, but I could have sworn he was speaking directly to us.

From there, we studied the Azusa Street Revival, the Los Angeles offshoot of the Wales experience, and then the spread thirty years later of Youth for Christ, which wasn't an organization or a ministry as much as it was a rallying cry for an entire generation of students who stood up to the prevailing agnostic beliefs of the day and said, "Christianity is not dead. God is not dead. Jesus is alive! He'll help you come to life too."

We talked about the Jesus Movement of the 1970s, about how businessmen and women in Southern California would come home after a long day at work and find random people swimming in the pool in their backyard. In response to the predictable questions—"Uh, who are you, and what are you doing in my pool?"—the swimmers would bubble over with enthusiasm and respond, "We just gave our lives to Jesus! We hopped the fence because we needed a place to get baptized!" Never mind there was an entire ocean a few miles west of the pool; it was an exciting time for anyone who was excitable. Jesus was on the scene.

In 1972, Campus Crusade for Christ hosted Explo '72 in Dallas, Texas, and by the end of the week-long conference aimed at training and equipping servants for Christ, more than three hundred thousand people had mobbed the Cotton Bowl, eager to more fully devote themselves to Christ. It was at this event that contemporary Christian music—a.k.a. "Jesus music"—was born.[56] Of all the high-profile bands that performed, I'd have wanted to see headliner Johnny Cash the most. At the close of the rally, the lights were dimmed and Billy Graham lighted a candle as he called a generation to live unashamed for Jesus. As that flame spread to the candles of ten, fifty, one hundred, and then nearly one hundred thousand people, calls came in to the Dallas Fire Department that the Cotton Bowl was on fire. While the fire department wasn't needed that night, the analysis was correct: the Cotton Bowl was on fire that night.

We would read all of the accounts of these and dozens more revivals/movements/experiences and come away shaking our heads. Just imagine if that kind of thing happened today, community after community being turned beautifully right side up—a total Jesus Revolution, in our cities, in our midst.

The Key to Every Revival

Of all the revivals my friends and I studied, the one I couldn't quit thinking about was the Welsh Revival. And the more I dug into it, the more I realized the legit role a guy named Evan Roberts played in its success. Evan was by most standards still a kid—twenty-six years old—when he rose to prominence as a preacher, maybe because young men worked the coal mines back then until they were in their early twenties or beyond. In many ways, at age twenty-six, Evan's life was only beginning, and he wanted it to begin strong.

Evan was so impacted by word of the church services being held in New Quay that he decided to enroll in seminary near his family's home in Wales. As the New Quay effect started to spread, Evan knew he wanted to experience one of the services for himself. He went to the seminary's principal and asked if he and a few of his friends could ditch classes for a week so that they could travel back to New Quay and hear the preacher preach firsthand. The (obviously cool) principal said, "You will learn more in a week of revival than in a year of seminary. Go."

At the revival, the preacher prayed that the people—himself included—would be "bent" toward the Lord. "Bend us toward you," he said, over and over again. Evan, for one, was bent. He returned to school, but only to ask for more time off. He wanted to go home and preach to his family's church, to the students who didn't know God, but he'd never preached before and had only three weeks of seminary training under his belt. The pastor of his home church wasn't convinced this was a good idea. "You can speak at the Monday-night prayer meeting," he told Evan, in effect muting the kid. Nobody ever went to that prayer meeting.

Seventeen people showed up the following Monday night, and with all the passion of a kid who doesn't care that he's unqualified for the job he's doing, Evan marched to the front of the room and said, "Let us pray." He prayed that the people would confess any known sin to God. He prayed that they would right any wrong that had been done to another person. He prayed that they would put away bad habits. He prayed that they would profess their faith publicly. And to no shock of Evan's, some of them actually did. The budding evangelist was invited to come back on Tuesday night.

By the end of that week, Evan had requested and received a second week off from seminary and was preaching every time his church's doors were open.

From there, he migrated to churches in neighboring communities, never announcing where he'd be, never promoting himself, simply showing up, taking the pulpit, and saying, "Let us pray." Night after night, Evan prayed, and night after night, new converts were made. Those converts then told their story of being lost and then found, being blind but now being able to see, which caused even more people to respond to Christ, until upward of one hundred thousand people in the UK alone had been saved, all because one guy decided to pray. For six years, Evan had prayed for this revival, he would later explain. And specifically, based on a vision he'd received from God, for those one hundred thousand souls. When God's people pray, God moves. Any time revival has shown up, somebody somewhere has prayed. I say let's be that somebody somewhere today.

Let Us Pray

Throughout history, the pattern for revival has always been the same. First, an individual or a small group of people gets frustrated with the state of affairs in their world. They see brokenness and rebellion and no worthwhile solution in sight. And so, they gather together to pray, which is step two in revival's course. They pray that the world would turn from their wickedness and turn toward God, and that God would bless them as a result. The Bible promises this is what happens, incidentally, when people quit sinning and start surrendering to him. "If . . . my people . . . respond [to me]," God says, "by humbling themselves, praying, seeking my presence, and turning their backs on their wicked lives, I'll be there ready for you: I'll listen from heaven, forgive their sins, and restore their land to health" (2 Chronicles 7:14).

When PULSE was just getting off the ground, we would tell students at our school that if they wanted to see our campus changed for good, they needed to start with prayer. We told them to go back to their individual groups and figure out the needs that should be met, and to their credit, they did just that. Business majors surveyed the landscape of the business school, art majors looked closely at the others' lives in their field, sorority girls paid attention to where their sorority sisters were hurting, and on and on it went. We prayed and God moved.

One time, two of my friends became passionate about reaching our campus for Jesus and happened to be construction management majors. They and a few other believers in their department had gathered to pray for their fellow students for several weeks when the idea hit them: they could raise money to host a free barbecue for the entire construction-management department, and then use that forum to tell people about a Bible study they were starting on campus the following week. What starving kid doesn't like free food? In the end fifty kids showed up, and thirty of them responded to Jesus.

I tell students still today, "Start at home. Does anybody in your family need Jesus? Start there. Then, look around you, right where you are. Who has a locker next to yours? What about the guy you sit next to in math class? The lady who always makes your Americano just right? The guy who cuts your hair? Start where you are, and work outward from there." There are people in your life I could never in a million years reach, and there are people in my life who will never cross paths with you. You are strategic to the plans of God. I am strategic to the plans of God. On any given day, we might be the answer to someone's prayers for rescue or hope. We might be the life preserver God tosses their way. As we begin to pray for the people in our life to know Jesus, more often than not God taps us on the shoulder and invites us to be part of his answer to that prayer.

The reason that prayer must be the precursor to seeing any movement of God is that prayer is the only way we get a lead on what he's up to. We can bang our heads against the wall of our strategies and our plans and our schemes all day long, but unless God is in those activities, our work will bear zero fruit. But on the flip side, there is much to be gained when we work in concert with him. "Don't hold back," 1 Corinthians 15:58 says. "Throw yourselves into the work of the Master, confident that nothing you do for him is a waste of time or effort." I am constantly challenged that what my situation needs isn't better ideas, some kind of brainstorming session with the world's elite. What my situation needs is divine intervention. The kind that only comes through prayer.

And what, exactly, is the "work of the Master" that's referenced in 1 Corinthians? It's his children, walking by faith. It's people in bondage, at last set free. It's loners, enfolded in community. It's rebels, welcomed home.

God's work is self-hatred transformed into acceptance.

It is unity where division once was.

It is beauty bursting through the ashes.

It is above all else marked by love.

As we devote ourselves to joining Jesus in his healing, freeing, transformative work, we reset our entire generation, one godly act at a time.

Along these lines, a pastor here in Minneapolis named John Piper once introduced me to a great grid for prayer. He called it the IOUs, and it goes like this:

- Incline my heart to you, not to prideful gain or any false motive. (Psalm 119:36)
- Open my eyes to behold wonderful things in your Word. (Psalm 119:18)
- Unite my heart to fear your name. (Psalm 86:11)
- Satisfy me with your steadfast love. (Psalm 90:14)[57]

I love this approach because it keeps me from rattling off a list of self-serving wants before God and coming away thinking I've prayed. It helps me stay focused on pursuing the Master's work instead of my own and, more specifically, on the Master himself. Incline my heart toward you, God; bend me to your will. Open my eyes to the truth of Scripture, so that the lies I'm believing will be exposed. Unite my heart to live today totally in awe of you. Satisfy me with your matchless love, so that I can quit looking for love everywhere else.

If you are frustrated with the hopelessness and helplessness you see surrounding you and want to be the somebody somewhere who catalyzes radical change, then I challenge you to start praying that IOUs prayer each day. When you come to God with open hands, an open heart, and an attitude of total surrender to his work, you'd better strap in and hold on tight. You're in for a wild ride.

Big Dream, Big God

In 2003, before PULSE started, before I'd written that paper to present to my English class, before I had any clear sense of what God was going to do with my life, I was working at Famous Dave's BBQ. I still remember the spiel I was expected to deliver to each new set of guests: "Good evening! Welcome to Famous Dave's! I'm Famous Nick! Can I get you a Famous margarita? A Famous Diet Coke? Some Famous Rib Tips to start you off?" I stuck to that script religiously, always terrified I was speaking to some secret shopper. Anyway, I was driving home from my Famous job one day, when I heard on the radio that Billy Graham was going to be in Oklahoma City the next night. I was in Fargo, as you'll recall, which is about thirteen hours north of OKC. Who cares; I had to go.

I raced home, changed clothes, grabbed a duffel bag, tossed in another pair of jeans and a toothbrush, and off I went. I had never heard Billy Graham speak live and knew that if I didn't go now, I may never have the chance. This guy was my hero, second only to my dad. Plus, being impulsive is one of my spiritual gifts. Of course I was going to go.

When God called me to tell people about Jesus as my life's work, I reread the entire Bible and then read Billy's autobiography, *Just as I Am,* four times through. (I met Tiffany shortly thereafter and remember saying to her, "Listen, Billy Graham was gone from his family 60 percent of the time. Can you handle that?" Nice and delicate, right? We hadn't even started dating yet. I'm sure she thought I was a little different.) I was enthralled by the stories Billy told about his early days as a traveling evangelist, about the team he'd surrounded himself with, and about God's faithfulness over the years. I wanted to see the entire operation firsthand, hoping for a few priceless tips.

En route to Oklahoma, I called around, trying to find a connection to someone who could get me tickets to the crusade. After one person pointed me to another person who pointed me to still another person working the event, I was somehow granted admittance into the Graham team's pre-event meetings. Billy Graham himself might be in that meeting. I drove faster thinking, *No way! No way! No* way!

I made my way to the hotel meeting room and slipped into the back so that I'd be out of the way. As I walked into the room, I felt like a spectator to living history. There was vocalist George Beverly Shea, and a few other official-looking men, and then Cliff Barrows, Billy's longtime emcee and music director. People had been chatting in small groups and administrative people had been tending to final details, making sure microphones were clipped in and water bottles were available, but as soon as Cliff started speaking, everyone was quiet. "I just met with Billy, and we are moved with the urgency for God to move tonight. We need to pray that God would change lives in this place," he said. And then, as a signal of his seriousness, he dropped to his knees to pray.

Now, Cliff Barrows had to have been late seventies, early eighties at the time. He was definitely old enough to make dropping to his knees a challenge. And yet there he was, kneeling on the floor of the meeting room, his head tilted heavenward, his arms spread wide. I couldn't help but stare. It was like God was saying, *Pay attention, Nick. This is why I bless these guys, because their hearts are fully mine.*

I stood there in awe. Given the reputation of these crusades, Billy and his team could have hit autopilot and coasted through the whole deal night after night. *The masses will come to Jesus no matter what we do,* they could have thought. *Pump up the song "Just as I Am," and they'll flood the altars like they always do!* And yet that's not at all what they did. They gathered together and prayed. They insisted on seeking God's face. And God blessed them time and again, like he promises he always will.

I wound up shadowing a bunch of people for the event: I worked on the field, I helped counsel those coming forward, and I even recommitted my life to Jesus. I did! As soon as that famous song started playing, I stood up and went right to the makeshift altar with tears streaming down my face. I totally surrendered to Jesus again, there at a Graham crusade. When the event ended and the crowds dispersed and Billy's crew started packing up all the gear, I found a seat in the back of that emptying stadium and prayed, *God, I want to do this with my life. This doesn't even make sense! But this is what I want to do.* God had been calling me into his work, and now I saw it for what it was. I was going to spend the rest of my days asking people to respond to Jesus.

At the time, the dream felt way too big for me—I mean, who gets to do something like what Billy Graham has done? And yet the more I prayed, the more I believed that if God was calling me, he would open the doors.

Fast-forward seven or eight years, and in the fall of 2010, my friends and I were busier than ever with PULSE events. God had been working in our team's hearts, and we all were praying harder, fasting more faithfully, and being stretched in our spiritual growth. One of the guys I had met at that Billy Graham Crusade, Jay, became not only a friend of mine but also a teammate, and on a drive from Milwaukee back to Minneapolis during that busy PULSE season, I told him that I wanted to do more, to go faster, to reach more kids with the message of Jesus.

For PULSE back then, a busy year equated to three full-scale seasons of outreach unfolding in different cities, which felt like a ton. But still, during different seasons of his ministry, Billy and his team were doing twenty or thirty events a year. I wasn't trying to be competitive with Billy Graham. I simply figured that if God had done it with one person, then he was more than capable of doing it with another.

Jay and I kept talking and then started praying, while cruising up the interstate. "God, give us thirty cities," he and I prayed, having no idea what we were asking for. "Multiply our efforts!" we said. "Help us reach more people for you."

Two weeks later, my phone rang. The guy on the other end said, "Hey, I heard about you from Billy Graham's team. We're launching a fifty-city tour, where ten thousand people will be gathered each night to hear about God. We want you to come share the gospel each of those nights. What do you think?"

Yeah, right. Hilarious, dude.

I was twenty-nine years old, the same age Billy Graham was when God plugged him into the biggest dream the guy had ever had. In that moment, as I realized this was no joke and that I wasn't being punked, it was like God said to me, *So, Nick. I'll see your thirty cities and add twenty. You in?*

Yeah, I was in. I was totally, ecstatically in.

A big dream requires a big God, and God was showing me how big he was. Over the year to come, our tour reached six hundred and fifty thousand people, and I signed up for that tour three years in a row. The wild ride I mentioned earlier? It was that, at about Mach 5.

Jesus Changes Everything

To stay in shape during those long tour seasons when a tour bus would deliver us from one nondescript city to the next day after day, night after night, week after grueling week, I'd show up early at the empty stadium where our event would be held and run the stairs. I'd stick in my earbuds, crank up some music, and run as fast as I could, making the same request of God that Cliff Barrows had made all those years before: *Move mightily tonight, God. Do it. Do it again in this place.* I wanted to touch every stair and pray for each person who would come that night.

One afternoon, after I'd been running up and down, up and down, for thirty minutes or so, a strange feeling came over me. I stopped in the middle of the aisle, tugged my earbuds out, and took in my surroundings. Where was I—Cleveland? Dallas? They all had started looking the same.

A guy was sweeping out a row a few aisles over. I turned his way and hollered, "Excuse me? What city is this?" to which he grinned and said, "Oklahoma City, pal. The one and only."

Oklahoma City. So that's why things felt familiar. I was in the very same venue where I'd been nine years prior, when I'd heard Billy Graham speak. Standing a few hundred feet from where I had sat in prayer for God to use my life, I was in absolute awe. That night, before a packed arena, the same exact place that Billy Graham had packed out before, I shared the good news of the gospel and invited people to respond to Jesus. And I marveled at God's goodness to me.

Astoundingly, things got even better from there. PULSE grew exponentially across America and internationally. I spent three years speaking on Winter Jam while also hosting festival events for the Luis Palau and Billy Graham associations, and it was during that mind-blowing season when I'd been invited to meet with Mr. Graham at his home in Montreat, North Carolina. By this time I was pretty good friends with his grandson, Will. Ahead of what I was sure would be a life-altering meeting with Billy Graham, I asked Will, "So, if I go in there and grab him by the ankle and beg him to give me The Blessing, will he freak out or be cool?"

Will just smiled. He'd seen people lose their better judgment in the face of his pillar of a grandfather before. "We have security ready for people like you, Nick."

During that Montreat meeting, Mr. Graham leaned in with wide eyes as

I shared the vision to fill the National Mall for Together 2016, and I thought maybe he and I would hop into the Jesus Mobile together right then and there! As I asked every single question I could think of, Mr. Graham graciously responded with variations on the same truth: "Jesus," he'd say. "It's all about Jesus. Spend time with Jesus, Nick. Spend time with him." I had once heard of someone commenting critically to Billy Graham, "I heard you twenty years ago, and you gave the same message as you did tonight." To them, apparently this seemed some kind of laziness. But not to Billy. "Thank you," was his reply. "I only have one message to give: Come to Jesus." As I sat there, I experienced the same simple truth. Our human wisdom will come to the end of itself at some point, but the wisdom of Jesus? It's always in plentiful supply.

On the way home from North Carolina, I reflected on my life to that point and realized that every good decision of consequence I'd ever made could be traced back to Jesus. Giving myself to him, giving up habits and tendencies that weren't bringing me life, speaking up for him even when it felt awkward at best, asking Tiffany to say yes, going all-in with PULSE, turning away from temptations time and again, trusting him with my days and with my past and with my dreams—everything right I'd ever done was explainable only in terms of him. *"Spend time with Jesus, Nick. Spend time with him."* If I only remember one lesson from this life, I sure hope that's the one.

It's Jesus who brings life and light.

It's Jesus who ushers in hope.

It's Jesus who defeated death and despair.

It's Jesus who wins in the end.

Let's Go All-In Together

One of my favorite parts of doing PULSE events is the moment when we offer students, parents, pastors, and other leaders to go all-in with us in reaching their community. In essence, we are saying, "We will match our faith with your faith. We are in if you are." Which brings me to my question for you: *Are you all-in?*

No matter what month or year it is as your eyes scan this page, there has never been a more exciting moment to live for Jesus than *right now.* The time for you to go all-in is now. Not tomorrow. Not next week. Not when you are ready, fixed, or better. You will never be ready, because this isn't about you. It's about the One who paved the way for you, and he is ready, willing, and able to match you, faith for faith. He is the answer, and he is calling your name. It is no coincidence that you are reading these words. Why? Because he's calling you home.

My prayer for you—for our entire generation—is that you would surrender fully. Invite Jesus into the mix-up of beauty and chaos and laughter and tears that is your life. Give him the all-access pass—your affections, your habits, your plans, your relationships, your everything—and tell him you're going all-in. Ask for and accept his forgiveness for anything that has been tripping you up. Don't let anything questionable become a stumbling block in your life. Take your eyes off of the bullying, the backbiting, the sin and substance abuse, the self-harm, the racial tension, the religious divides, the selfishness, the apathy, the rage . . . all the things that threaten to take our generation down. And put your eyes on Jesus, the One who alone can intervene. Say yes to Jesus right now. "Today is the day of salvation," says 2 Corinthians 6:2 (NLT). "Now is the right time to listen, the day to be helped," the apostle Paul says. "Don't put it off; don't frustrate God's work by showing up late, throwing a question mark over everything we're doing" (verse 3).

"Why is today the right day to respond?" you may ask. Why *not* today? Can you think of one good reason why you would not give your life to the One who changes everything? An old-school evangelist named Lowell Lundstrom once encouraged me to tell people, "Give all your sins to Jesus. Surrender everything to him and let him lead your life. If you don't like it, you can have all your sins back." What he was saying is that you have *nothing* to lose here and all of eternity to gain. There is a reset waiting for you, and today can be the day you say yes.

The vision for Together 2016 came about for this very reason—because we're all in need of a reset. We're all worn out from solutions that can't deliver. We're all searching for that missing piece to pull our lives together. I believe God asked us to rally the nation on the National Mall for Together 2016 to spread one message loud and clear: "Jesus is the answer." The answer isn't a four-step process, event, or program. The answer is a person. No matter what the question is, its answer is found in him.

Who should we follow? Jesus.

Who is a trustworthy leader? Jesus.

What is the way out of this unbelievable mess we've made? Jesus.

Who saves? Jesus.

Who cares? Jesus.

Where is love really found? Jesus.

This is more than a Sunday school answer. This is the gospel in one name: *Jesus.* Jesus changes everything.

The answer to any worthwhile question you can ask is Jesus—and him, alone. This is why we planned the gathering on our nation's capital, our eyes fixed on the same prize—and why PULSE is still rallying people around the world today. We gather because we are done running and done being defined by division and judgment rather than life and love. We lift our voices as one in surrender, asking for a generation-defining moment, that we might be reset to be the people he created us to be. In the words that close the New Testament, our voices and our hearts declare, "'Come, Master Jesus!' We wait for you alone."

Come, Lord Jesus. Reset this generation. And let it start with me.

Acknowledgments

Working on this book has been an amazing process that wouldn't have happened without a team. Thank you to Ashley Wiersma for believing in me and investing your time and energy into this project. You are the best.

Lisa Jackson, without your belief in me and in PULSE, this book wouldn't be getting out. Thanks to you and the team at Alive.

Thanks to Susan, Alex, and the team at Multnomah for taking on *Reset* and helping us spread the story to as many as possible.

To Sharon Sampson and Team Open Book, thanks for helping us find our story.

To the team at PULSE, thank you for your work and dedication to see this generation awakened to the reality of Jesus. Chris, Justin, Jay, and Susan, you make up the best leadership team I've ever been on and are some of my best friends. Thank you Camden for your help editing, Boda for your inspiration and encouragement, Jeff and Karen for your wisdom, Jenah and Lenea for your baby-sitting, and Nanda for your design work.

To Laurel, Jadi, Troy, Mike, Renee, Fern, Blaise, Mark, Brad, Seth, Rich, Ralph, Chuck, Chris, Justin, and Dabbs, thanks for being not only board members but friends.

Thank you Troy Easton, Jordan Halvorsen, Cindy Stadum, Jenn Porter, Eden Meyer, Josh Keller, Matt Best, Carl Larsen, Cody Redmer, Dan Bruns, and every early staff member for your blood, sweat, and tears to get PULSE off the ground.

To the students leaders, campus staff, and supporters during those first years of PULSE events at ND State, Concordia, MSUM, VC State, Jamestown, BSU, U Mary, Mayville, Minot, Bemidji, and UND, this is your story every bit as much as it is mine.

To Mike Montgomery, thanks for being a friend, big brother, and mentor.

To Shane Stacey, Sammy Wanyonyi, Dave Gibson, Joaquin Vargas, Dave Lubben, Matthew St. John, Troy Easton, Paul Persen, Lance Thorson, Matt Rusten, Skip Johnson, Ben Meland, and Troy Nelson, thanks for being brothers who hold me accountable to my faith, family, and calling.

To Governor Ed and Nancy Schafer, Senator John and Mikey Hoeven, and Congressman Kevin and Kris Cramer, for your support of the next generation.

To Warren Waind, Russ Irwin, Ray Anderson, Doug Anderson, Andy Veith, Luis Palau, Dave Jones, Kevin Palau, Alan Hotchkiss, John Ogle, Tim Robnett, Sandra Barrett, Reid Saunders, Jose Zayas, York Moore, Bob Lenz, Keith Cook, Paul Hendricks, Tony Nolan, Eddie Carswell, Jake Carswell, Johnny Hunt, Fern Nichols, Paul Cedar, Doug Birdsall, Dimas Salaberrios, Josh McDowell, Steven Douglass, Francis Chan, JW Clarke, Gary Cobb, John Cass, Dan Klug, Troy and Kree Nelson, Brad and Kathy Miller, Mark and Kim Thompson, Steve and Patty White, Mike and Kim Slette, Ken and LuAnn Regan, Larry and Julie Leitner, and the countless others who believed in, prayed for, invested in, rebuked on behalf of, encouraged, and opened doors for me.

To Dad, you are my hero.

To Mom, you are my prayer warrior and confidant.

To Jennie, you are the best sister ever.

To Billy, you are my brother, friend, and the coolest person I know.

To Tiffany, you are my best friend and no one deserves my gratitude more. I love you.

To Jesus, you are my Savior and Lord. As with all stories worth telling, this one is yours.

Notes

1. Matthew 5:11–12.
2. Check out the full story in Judges 6–8.
3. Switchfoot, "Meant to Live," *The Beautiful Letdown,* copyright © 2003, Columbia, Sony BMG.
4. "How Much Do College Students Drink?," 12 Keys Rehab (blog), December 17, 2013, www.12keysrehab.com/blog/How-Much-Do-College-Students-Drink.
5. Michelle Castillo, "Survey reveals shocking levels of teen drinking, drug abuse," CBS News, April 3, 2012, www.cbsnews.com/news/survey-reveals-shocking-levels-of-teen-drinking-drug-abuse.
6. Chiara Sabina, Janis Wolak, and David Finkelhor, "The Nature and Dynamics of Internet Pornography Exposure for Youth," *Cyber Psychology and Behavior* 11, no. 6 (2008): 2, doi: 10.1089/cpb.2007.0179, www.unh.edu/ccrc/pdf/CV169.pdf.
7. Barna Group, "Six Reasons Young Christians Leave Church," Research Release in Millennials and Generations, September 27, 2011, www.barna.org/barna-update/millennials/528-six-reasons-young-christians-leave-church#.Voc1qfkrLIU.
8. Office of Statistics and Programming, National Center for Injury Prevention and Control, Centers for Disease Control, "10 Leading Causes of Death by Age Group, United States, 2010," www.cdc.gov/injury/wisqars/pdf/10LCID_All_Deaths_By_Age_Group_2010-a.pdf.
9. Kalman Heller, "Depression in Teens and Children," *PsychCentral,* March 15, 2012, http://psychcentral.com/lib/depression-in-teens-and-children.
10. Spotify is a digital music service, in case you don't run in Millennial circles.

11. Weeknd, "The Hills," *Beauty Behind the Madness,* copyright © 2015, XO, Republic.
12. Fetty Wap, "679," *Fetty Wap,* copyright © 2015, RGF, 300.
13. Drake, "Hotline Bling," *Views from the 6,* copyright © 2015, Cash Money, Republic.
14. OMI, "Cheerleader," *Me 4 U,* copyright © 2012, Oufah, Ultra, Columbia.
15. Macklemore and Ryan Lewis, "Downtown," *Downtown,* copyright © 2015, Macklemore.
16. Lady Gaga, "Beautiful, Dirty, Rich," *The Fame,* copyright © 2008, Streamline, Kon Live, Cherrytree, Interscope.
17. Ke$ha, "Tik Tok," *Animal,* copyright © 2009, RCA.
18. TLC, "Let's Do It Again," *CrazySexyCool,* copyright © 1994, LaFace, Arista.
19. Far East Movement, "Life a G6," *Free Wired,* copyright © 2010, Cherrytree.
20. Avril Lavigne, "What the Hell," *Goodbye Lullaby,* copyright © 2011, RCA.
21. John Mayer, "Who Says," *Battle Studies,* copyright © 2009, Columbia.
22. Katy Perry, "Teenage Dream," *Teenage Dream,* copyright © 2010, Capitol.
23. The Rolling Stones, "(I Can't Get No) Satisfaction," *Out of Our Heads,* copyright © 1965, Decca.
24. Daniel Schorn, "Transcript: Tom Brady, Part 3—Tom Brady Talks to Steve Kroft," *60 Minutes,* November 4, 2005, www.cbsnews.com/news/transcript-tom-brady-part-3.
25. Dotson Rader, "The Mixed-Up Life of Shia LaBeouf," *Parade,* June 14, 2009, http://parade.com/130832/dotsonrader/shia-labeouf-mixed-up-life.
26. Linkin Park, "Waiting for the End," *A Thousand Suns,* copyright © 2010, Warner Bros.
27. Three Days Grace, "The Good Life," *Life Starts Now,* copyright © 2010, Jive.
28. Bruno Mars, "Grenade," *Doo-Wops & Hooligans,* copyright © 2010, Elektra.
29. U2, "I Still Haven't Found What I'm Looking For," *The Joshua Tree,* copyright © 1987, Island.
30. Scott McConnell, "LifeWay Research Finds Reasons 18- to 22-Year-Olds Drop Out of Church," Lifeway, August 7, 2007, www.lifeway.com/Article/LifeWay-Research-finds-reasons-18-to-22-year-olds-drop-out-of-church.

31. See Matthew 21:12–13.
32. Roger E. Olson, "Did Karl Barth Really Say " 'Jesus Loves Me, This I Know . . . ?' " *Patheos,* January 24, 2013, www.patheos.com/blogs/rogereolson/2013/01/did-karl-barth-really-say-jesus-loves-me-this-i-know.
33. A. B. Simpson, *Millennial Chimes: A Collection of Poems* (New York: Christian Alliance, 1894), 28.
34. "Jim Elliot Quote," Billy Graham Center, Archives, last revised May 31, 2012, www2.wheaton.edu/bgc/archives/faq/20.htm.
35. J. F. X. O'Conor, *A Study of Francis Thompson's Hound of Heaven* (New York: John Lane, 1912), 28.
36. The hilarious footnote to the story is that on the heels of Jesus' healing the madman, some people in town demand for Jesus to leave. Why, you ask? Because he sent the evil spirits into the herd of pigs and those pigs ran off a cliff. What? This story is officially awesome. The zombie-hulk-demonic-bacon pigs just went cliff jumping! Tell me again that Jesus is boring, I dare you.
37. Hillsong United, "Arise," *Zion,* copyright © 2013, Sparrow.
38. Fergie, "Glamorous," *The Dutchess,* copyright © 2007, A&M, will.i.am, Interscope.
39. Nickelback, "Rockstar," *All the Right Reasons,* copyright © 2006, Roadrunner.
40. Usher, "I Don't Know," *8701,* copyright © 2001, Arista.
41. For more on this subject, Google "one anothers in Scripture."
42. "Sexual Risk Behaviors: HIV, STD, and Teen Pregnancy Prevention," Centers for Disease Control and Prevention, www.cdc.gov/healthyyouth/sexualbehaviors.
43. Rob Jackson, "When Children View Pornography," Focus on the Family, 2004, www.focusonthefamily.com/parenting/sexuality/when-children-use-pornography/when-children-view-pornography. See also Rebecca L. Collins, Steven C. Martino, and Rebecca Shaw, "Influence of New Media on Adolescent Sexual Health: Evidence and Opportunities," Rand Health working paper, US Department of Health and Human Services, Washington, DC, April 15, 2011, https://aspe.hhs.gov/basic-report/influence-new-media-adolescent-sexual-health-evidence-and-opportunities.

44. T.I., "Dead and Gone," featuring Justin Timberlake, *Paper Trail,* copyright © 2008, Grand Hustle, Atlantic.
45. Leonard Cohen, "Anthem," *Live in London,* copyright © 2009, Columbia Records.
46. Amy Winehouse, "Rehab," *Back to Black,* copyright © 2006, Universal Records.
47. See Gary Smalley and John Trent, *The Two Sides of Love* (Carol Stream, IL: Tyndale, 2005).
48. Sheree Johnson, "New Research Sheds Light on Daily Ad Exposures," SJ Insights, September 29, 2014, http://sjinsights.net/2014/09/29/new-research-sheds-light-on-daily-ad-exposures.
49. See 1 Timothy 1:15, KJV.
50. Arnold Cole and Pamela Caudill Ovwigho, "Understanding the Bible Engagement Challenge: Scientific Evidence for the Power of 4," Center for Bible Engagement, December 2009, www.centerforbibleengagement.org/images/stories/pdf/Scientific_Evidence_for_the_Power_of_4.pdf.
51. See Luke 6:35, NIV.
52. L. B. Cowman, *Streams in the Desert: 366 Daily Devotional Readings,* ed. James Reimann (Grand Rapids, MI: Zondervan, 1997), 390.
53. See Matthew 19 for the full story, beginning in verse 16.
54. Hillsong United, "One Pure and Holy Passion," *Passion: One Day Live,* copyright © 2000, Sparrow.
55. J. Edwin Orr, "The Awakening of 1904 in Wales," History of Revival Series, preached in 1981 at Church on the Way, Van Nuys, California, www.jedwinorr.com/resources/audio/COW_08.MP3.
56. Larry Eskridge, "The 'Praise and Worship' Revolution," *Christian History,* October 29, 2008, www.christianitytoday.com/ch/thepastinthepresent/storybehind/praiseworshiprevolution.html.
57. Jonathan Parnell, "One Way to Avoid Vain Repetition," *DesiringGod,* October 19, 2010, www.desiringgod.org/articles/one-way-to-avoid-vain-repetition.

Printed in the United States
by Baker & Taylor Publisher Services